CONTENTS

trotman

GETTING INTO

American
Universities

Margaret Kroto

About the Author

Margaret Kroto has been a careers practitioner for 35 years, 23 of these as the careers information and publications manager for a careers company. During this time she has produced many local publications and written articles for national directories. She has lived, worked and travelled extensively in North America.

Thanks to all the students who provided useful tips.

Getting into American Universities
This first edition published in 2004 by Trotman and Company Ltd
2 The Green, Richmond, Surrey TW9 1PL

The information in this book was correct at the time of going to press. However, as details may change at any time, it is always advisable to check with the original source.

Editorial and Publishing Team
Author Margaret Kroto
Editorial Mina Patria, Editorial Director; Rachel Lockhart, Commissioning Editor; Anya Wilson, Managing Editor; Bianca Knights, Assistant Editor
Production Ken Ruskin, Head of Pre-press and Production; James Rudge, Production Assistant
Sales and Marketing Deborah Jones, Head of Sales and Marketing
Advertising Tom Lee, Commercial Director
Managing Director Toby Trotman

British Library Cataloguing in Publication Data
A catalogue record for this book is available from the British Library

ISBN 0 85660 978 1

Typeset by Mac Style Ltd, Scarborough, N. Yorkshire
Printed and bound in Great Britain by Bell & Bain Ltd, Glasgow, Scotland

INTRODUCTION

The American higher education system is quite different from that of the UK in a number of important respects. This book is designed to provide information for individuals who are considering this route, and their advisers and teachers. The main focus is on choosing and getting into undergraduate programmes, but sections on exchange programmes and postgraduate courses are included as these are excellent alternatives for which some form of funding is more likely to be available. Many of the graduate students interviewed felt that it was a great pity that so few British students were aware of the extensive opportunities for postgraduate study and would like to see these more widely publicised.

The United States government and many university admissions departments have been concerned that recent events have discouraged students from choosing to study there as the number of student visa applications dropped dramatically after the terrorist events of 11 September 2001 ('9/11'). Maura Harty, Assistant Secretary of State for Consular Affairs, issued the following statement:

'Foreign students have always been – and still are – welcome to study in the United States. The tragedy of 9/11 showed the importance of emphasizing national security, but that does not mean we want to discourage legitimate students from coming here to study. We value the diversity and richness they bring to American campuses and society. Although long-standing visa laws and regulations are followed rigorously, and new visa procedures have been introduced since 9/11, the impact on students is always carefully considered.'

(Source: The Fulbright Commission website which carries the full text – www.fulbright.co.uk)

None of the students interviewed for this book had any reservations about the choice they had made. If you are well prepared and well informed you are more likely to make a sound choice.

Good luck!

With thanks to students, admissions and international service staff at Florida State University, the University of California at Berkeley, Santa Barbara and Los Angeles, and Stanford University.

Part I

UNDERGRADUATE STUDY

1

WHY STUDY IN THE USA?

There are many attractions to studying in another country, and the USA is a popular choice for English-speaking students as there is no language barrier. If you take the time to investigate all the options thoroughly and are aware of all the implications, particularly financial, you will be able to make a realistic and positive decision. You will need to start the process earlier than you would for a course in the UK as it takes time to gather the information, make your choice, or choices, of course and institution, complete the application procedure and then apply for your visa once you have been accepted. It is recommended that you apply at least a year in advance, but individual institutions will have different requirements.

SOME ADVANTAGES
- You will experience a different culture and lifestyle.
- You will have a very broad education and often a wider choice of options.

- You will have a very wide choice of institutions and courses.
- You will experience a different system of education.
- Entry to some colleges may be possible with five GCSE/Standard Grade passes.
- Some courses are not available in the UK.
- It is not difficult to change your choice of major subject in the first two years.
- Americans are generally friendly and welcoming.
- The climate may be more appealing in some areas (e.g. California).
- It could give you an advantage if you wish to live in the USA and your area of expertise is in demand.
- If you are a top athlete or especially gifted you could get a scholarship.

POSSIBLE DISADVANTAGES/ OTHER CONSIDERATIONS

- Undergraduate courses normally take four years in the United States and you may find that you have already covered some of the work done in the first two years.
- Regardless of your qualifications you must normally reach a specified level in Verbal and Maths tests – the Scholastic Assessment Test (SAT) or the American College Test (ACT). Some institutions will require subject tests (SAT II).
- You will have regular homework and assignments and be required to attend all lectures.
- It is very expensive for international students, even in public institutions.
- You will need a student visa which may not be renewed if you are not progressing.
- Students can sometimes be delayed for long periods on entry to the USA.
- There is no national health system and insurance is a mandatory extra.
- It will be more difficult and expensive to get home in an emergency.
- Some campuses are extremely large and this may not suit everyone.
- Although you may work on campus, authorisation documents may take some time.

■ Law, medicine and dentistry are postgraduate courses in the USA.

■ You may not wish to study subjects you left behind after GCSEs or Standard Grades.

■ There are no student bars on campus as the legal age for drinking alcohol is 21.

2

THE SYSTEM OF EDUCATION IN THE UNITED STATES

HIGH SCHOOLS The education system is quite different in the USA as students are required to study a broad range of subjects in order to graduate from high school. The high-school diploma is not based on a national examination system equivalent to A-levels, but awarded to students who successfully complete assignments and pass tests (mostly multiple choice) in a specified range of subjects. Students are continually evaluated and graded on their performance in tests, assignments, projects, class discussions, etc. Grades range from A (excellent) to F (fail). Most students graduate with a high-school diploma when they have completed Grade 12. The nearest equivalent in the UK is at least five GCSEs in a broad range of subjects, including Maths (known as 'Math' in the USA), English, a science, social science/humanities subject and a foreign language.

THE GRADING SYSTEM

Grades are awarded for each credit hour in the American system, both in high schools and in universities, so that it is important for students to attend classes to maintain their Grade Point Average (GPA).

Standard	Grade	Points
Excellent	A	4.00
	A-	3.75
Good	B+	3.25
	B	3.00
	B-	2.75
Average	C+	2.25
	C	2.00
	C-	1.75
Poor/minimal pass	D+	1.25
	D	1.00
	D-	0.75
Failure or Unsatisfactory	F or U	0.00

In cases of incomplete work, grade points are not awarded.

The interpretation of grades can vary slightly – at Drew University in New Jersey, for example, A- = 3.67 and B+ = 3.33, making these two grades closer together. Occasionally, a scale of 5 is used.

The GPA is calculated by dividing the total number of points by the number of credit hours taken. An overall minimum GPA of 2.00 is required to graduate from a university.

UNIVERSITIES

The system mirrors that of high schools, with continuous assessment and the building up of credits. It continues to be based on a broad range of subjects for the first two years of the degree programme, and students then concentrate on their chosen major subject for the final two years. Although you will normally be asked to choose a major subject when you apply, it is usually possible to change fairly easily during the first two years. Some institutions, including the very prestigious Stanford University, welcome outstanding students who are undecided about their major subject, as this is often an indication of all-round ability and an open mind. For international students, however, the US Educational Advisory Service in London recommends that for visa purposes, students should declare a major. Students must take a broad range of subjects, including Maths, English, a science subject, a language (which could be American Sign Language, if available and unless otherwise specified) and a humanities or social science subject. The first two years could, therefore, be considered to be broadly equivalent to an A-level course, but in a wider range of subjects. The first year could be considered to be equivalent to Higher and the second to Advanced Higher in the Scottish system. The curriculum for the first two years is frequently referred to as 'The Liberal Studies Program' and is designed to give breadth to a student's academic experience. Many universities operate a semester system, with most students completing two semesters a year and using the summer to take paid employment. It is usually possible to take courses in the summer semester if desired. Some universities use a 'quarter' system, dividing study periods into four terms.

3

CHOOSING A UNIVERSITY OR COLLEGE

The USA is a very large country, with some states being larger than Britain, and there are consequently many institutions to choose from. A high percentage of Americans do go on to college and there are more than 2,100 institutions listed in *Peterson's Four-Year Colleges*, one of the most widely used reference sources. Guides such as these provide information such as the courses offered, number of students, cost, entrance requirements, percentage of students with SAT Verbal and Maths scores above 600, percentage in the top 10% of their high school and the percentage of applicants accepted. This will help you to narrow down your choices by selecting schools which match your profile and are consequently more likely to be interested in your application. Do not be put off applying, however, if there is an institution you particularly want to attend, as you may be able to convince the admissions staff of your suitability and motivation.

Some universities offer summer sessions for students who would like to get a taste of study at that institution. Sessions are normally offered between May and August, and information on dates and costs can be found on websites or by direct application.

You should be aware that the United States government does not monitor the quality of US colleges and universities, but approves accrediting agencies. You must, therefore, make sure that any college you apply to is accredited by a recognised accrediting agency. Those included in the major college guides are recognised, and the US Educational Advisory Service (see Appendix 2, 'Sources of information') can also advise on this.

HOW SELECTIVE IS EACH INSTITUTION?

The following categories are commonly used in national directories to help students assess their chances of achieving a successful application:

- Most difficult (or highly competitive). These colleges are extremely selective and the majority of students will have achieved high test scores. *Ivy League colleges* such as Harvard and Princeton, and other prestigious institutions such as Stanford, come into this category, as do some of the more celebrated public institutions such as the University of California at Berkeley (UC Berkeley) and Los Angeles (UCLA). At these universities, more than 75% of freshmen will normally have been in the top 10% of their high-school class and scored more than 1310 in the SAT, or over 29 in the ACT. The acceptance rate is 30% or fewer applicants.
- Very difficult (or very competitive). These colleges also have many more applications than places, but should not be a problem for students predicted to get B and C grades at AS and A-levels, or A or B grades in Higher and Advanced Higher in Scotland. More than 50% of freshmen will normally have been in the top 10% of their high-school class and scored over 1230 in the SAT, or over 26 in the ACT. The acceptance rate is 60% or fewer applicants.
- Moderately difficult (or competitive). These colleges are less competitive and should present no problem to students likely to

get offers at less competitive universities in the UK. Over 75% of successful applicants will normally have been in the top half of their high school and scored over 1010 in the SAT and over 18 in the ACT. The acceptance rate is 85% or fewer applicants.

■ Minimally difficult (or less competitive). Normally, 95% of applicants will be accepted at these colleges, and most freshmen will not have been in the top half of their high school – their SAT combined score is likely to be below 1010, and the ACT below 19.

■ Non-competitive. A certain standard will be expected at these colleges, but access is otherwise fairly open.

When interpreting the above figures, you should remember that almost all Americans remain in high school until the age of 18, and it might be more meaningful to rate your position at the time of your GCSEs, or Standard Grade qualifications in Scotland. If, for example, the bottom 25% of the students in your school leave at the age of 16, it will subsequently become more difficult to be in the top 10% of the year. The SAT score quoted above is the combined Verbal and Maths score for SAT 1.

Unless you have specific reasons for choosing a particular location or college, you should consider a wide range of institutions and not just those that are well known internationally, as they tend to be highly selective and your chances of being admitted are slim unless you are an exceptional candidate. There are over 3,000 four-year colleges in the USA and, whilst the elite are inundated with well-qualified applicants, many others are competing for students. Many good colleges accept all students who fulfil the minimum academic requirements.

American universities tend to put a lot of emphasis on the 'student profile', and their websites will often provide an outline of the type of student that they feel will benefit most from the educational experience their particular institution offers. It is important to look at individual websites as they contain a great deal of essential information to help you to make your decision. You can request printed catalogues or directories, but there is often a charge for these, and similar information is on websites. There are priced services offering to make selections based on the criteria you specify, but if you are willing to take the time to do your own research, there is no reason why you should not make a sound choice without this additional expense. You could, however, take advantage of the annual US undergraduate fair, known as College Day, which usually takes place at the American School in London and is organised by the US Educational Advisory Service (EAS – see Appendix 2, 'Sources of information'). You should bear in mind that many American universities do not attend this event, but those that do are likely to be interested in recruiting from the UK as well as from American citizens attending the school.

TYPES OF UNIVERSITY AND COLLEGE

The terms 'university', 'college' and 'institution' are all used for degree-awarding institutions in the USA, and the term used has no bearing on quality or prestige. Some of the most prestigious institutions are liberal arts colleges or institutes. Universities are generally larger and made up of several schools.

PUBLIC UNIVERSITIES

Public universities are controlled by the state in which they are located and are often very large. Florida State University, for example, has almost 37,000 students, and others have numbers in the region of 50,000. Although the majority of undergraduates will be local due to the preferential fee structure, FSU, for example, has students from all the other states and 100 other countries. These larger campuses do, therefore, have a cosmopolitan atmosphere. Public institutions are prohibited from any religious affiliation by federal and state law. The state or public universities in the Midwest, west and south tend to be stronger as the first universities were all private and founded in the eastern states, where they have generally remained the most prestigious institutions. It can be more difficult for a good international student to get into a top public institution, as they are likely to be required by the state which funds them to give priority to qualified in-state students.

PRIVATE UNIVERSITIES

There are many private universities in the United States, including the most prestigious Ivy League group (see below). These institutions have the same fee structure, regardless of residence or nationality. They tend to be very expensive, but are also likely to have more open scholarships for which foreign nationals are eligible to apply. The top colleges attract gifted students from all over the world. Perhaps the most famous of these are the Ivy League universities, which tend to be regarded as the American equivalent of Oxford and Cambridge. They are very competitive. The eight Ivy League universities (all on the east coast) are Brown, Columbia, Cornell, Dartmouth, Harvard, Pennsylvania, Princeton and Yale. They are well-established institutions and are said to have got their name from the ivy plants which frequently grow on the sides of their magnificent old buildings. There are, however, many other prestigious private institutions outside this group. These include Stanford (California), MIT (Massachusetts Institute of Technology) and a number of liberal arts colleges.

AMERICAN COLLEGE CONFERENCE

Some regional groups of universities have formed themselves into special 'conferences' for the purposes of competition and cooperation. Inter-collegiate athletics is a significant and prominent aspect of these conferences. Inter-collegiate athletics is a very big thing in American universities and the most competitive are those most likely to offer scholarships to talented athletes. The Ivy League (see above) is one of these conferences. Other major conferences are The Big East, The Big Ten, The Pacific 10 and The Southeastern Conference. Conferences may be formed exclusively of private institutions, or a mixture of private and public. There are also small college partnerships (e.g. Massachusetts Five-College Consortium and Claremont Colleges in California), where smaller colleges pool their resources with a larger institution, or group together to form a larger body.

LIBERAL ARTS COLLEGES

Liberal arts colleges tend to be much smaller and can be very exclusive. A liberal arts education is a broad education and the term does not mean that students study only the arts and humanities. In fact, it is really a shortened form of 'liberal arts and sciences'; the curriculum is not very different from that of any other higher education institution and you can major in a similar range of subjects. Liberal arts colleges tend to sell themselves on the fact that they are smaller and more personal. You are likely to have a more sheltered life and to be very much part of a small community. These colleges are usually independent and many have excellent academic reputations. They may have religious affiliations.

SINGLE-SEX LIBERAL ARTS COLLEGES

There are now very few single-sex liberal arts colleges, and most are for women students. Some of the original group of very prestigious women's colleges, known as the 'Seven Sisters', have now merged with other institutions, including Radcliffe College, which merged with Harvard in 1999. Amongst the most elite of those that remain as women's colleges are Bryn Mawr (near Philadelphia), Mount Holyoke, Smith and Wellesley (all in Massachusetts). The latter now offers students the opportunity to join classes at MIT. Barnard College, a women's college in New York City, is affiliated to Columbia University (see Ivy League). Sweet Briar College in Virginia is another well-established women's college. Students at Mount Holyoke are required to live in college for all four undergraduate years and this will not suit everyone. Perhaps the best-known men's liberal arts college is Wabash College in Crawfordsville, Indiana. It has only 900 students, 30 of whom are international.

UNIVERSITIES WITH STRONG RELIGIOUS AFFILIATIONS

There are many universities with strong religious affiliations in the USA. They are always private and may be small colleges or universities such as the Protestant Pepperdine in Malibu, or larger institutions such as Brigham Young, the Mormon university in Salt Lake City. If you wish to look specifically at colleges with religious affiliations, you can search for these on www.a2zcolleges.com – it covers mainly Catholic, Protestant and Mormon institutions, and you can search by clicking on 'Religion', and then search the whole of the USA or a particular state.

HISTORICALLY BLACK CAMPUS UNIVERSITIES (HBCU) AND TRADITIONALLY WHITE INSTITUTIONS (TWI)

You will sometimes see institutions referred to as historically black or traditionally white, but of course all are now open to everyone who qualifies to study there. There is an association for Black American Colleges and Universities (BACU), whose policy it is to encourage black students to consider the range of institutions. It recognises, however, that some students may make a positive choice of a historically black institution, and publishes the names of these.

RESEARCH UNIVERSITIES

A few very prestigious institutions, such as California Institute of Technology (Caltech), are primarily geared towards postgraduate study in the sciences, but do take undergraduates. This is not an official category of university, but top students aiming at research careers may wish to know which universities have a very high percentage of postgraduate students, and which offer no postgraduate study or opportunities for undergraduate research projects. Universities with fewer undergraduates than postgraduates include Caltech, Stanford, Harvard and MIT. Large, highly competitive public universities, such as Berkeley and UCLA in California, also have a larger number of postgraduates than undergraduates. The vast majority of universities and colleges also offer research-based postgraduate courses, but have a higher number of undergraduate students. Some of these are very highly regarded in the research field, and you can generally recognise them by the large number of postgraduates they have (information on this can be found in reference books and on individual websites). You should, however, bear in mind that some small colleges have carried out some very successful research projects.

COMPREHENSIVE COLLEGES

The higher education guide produced by *US News* puts comprehensive colleges into a separate category, but most do not. Typically, they offer the usual wide range of courses, and some professional courses, such as Dental Hygiene, Nursing, and Physical Therapy (Physiotherapy), Education and Business, but many universities also offer these.

SPECIALIST COLLEGES

Whilst the majority of colleges offer a very wide range of courses, some either specialise in, or have developed a particular reputation for, a certain type of course or learning style. Examples are:

- ■ Art and design – California Institute of the Arts, Cooper Union, Parsons School of Design (both in New York), School of the Art Institute of Chicago, School of the Museum of Fine Arts (Boston) – in addition many major universities have strong reputations in this area.
- ■ Music – Juilliard School (New York), New England Conservatory of Music, Boston Conservatory, Manhattan School of Music, San Francisco Conservatory of Music – plus many major universities and liberal arts colleges.
- ■ Drama and Dance – New York University, Sarah Lawrence (New York), Princeton and UCLA (Los Angeles) are not specialist institutions, but are amongst those with outstanding reputations.
- ■ Film and television – many of those with outstanding schools are in the public sector and include Arizona State, Boston, Michigan State, NYU (New York), FSU (Tallahassee) and UCLA (Los Angeles). USC (University of Southern California – a very competitive private school in Los Angeles) also has an outstanding film school.
- ■ Technical institutes – Caltech, Colorado School of Mines, Florida Institute of Technology, Georgia Institute of Technology, Harvey Mudd College (California), MIT, Illinois Institute of Technology and many others.
- ■ Nonconformist colleges – amongst the best known are Antioch (Ohio), Hampshire and Sarah Lawrence (New York City).

The Fiske Guide to Getting into the Right College (see Appendix 2, 'Sources of information') provides information on specialist colleges, but no list is fully comprehensive, and the information is often subjective. If you do your research thoroughly, you may well find other colleges equally suitable for you. Websites are an excellent source of information. The website www.a2zcolleges.com allows you to search for drama schools, arts colleges and music schools.

COMMUNITY COLLEGES

Community colleges are non-competitive and usually attended by local students without the entry requirements for a four-year degree. They offer a variety of two-year courses, and successful students can transfer to a four-year programme at a university and obtain credits for study already completed. Universities in the state system are usually required to accept successful students who are residents of that state. In some cases, American citizens can be regarded as residents of a state when they have lived there for one year, but this does not apply to nationals of other countries, of course. Community colleges are an option for those students who do not have the minimum required qualifications and also tend to be cheaper.

TYPES OF UNDERGRADUATE COURSES

BACHELOR'S DEGREE

Most foreign nationals looking for a full-time undergraduate course in the USA will be thinking in terms of a Bachelor's degree (this may also be referred to as a Baccalaureate degree). As has already been stated, this provides a broad education for the first two years, and the study of a major subject for the final two years. Graduates are normally awarded a BA (arts and humanities subjects) or a BS (engineering and science subjects). A BFA (Bachelor of Fine Arts) may be awarded at some institutions for a few subjects, including performance arts. Degrees of distinction may be awarded as follows:

- Cum Laude – overall GPA of 3.50
- Magna Cum Laude – overall GPA of 3.70
- Summa Cum Laude – overall GPA of 3.90

In the UK system, the majority of students follow an Honours degree programme (e.g. BA (Hons), but the 'Honors Program' in American universities is normally one that academically talented students elect to follow if they are eligible. At some institutions you would be invited to apply as a freshman, and at others you could choose this option in your junior year if your GPA is above a specified level. Institutions may offer 'general' and 'specialized' honours programmes – it varies and you would need to enquire. To graduate with honours, you must achieve a specified overall GPA, and write and defend a thesis covering independent work you have done alongside your chosen courses.

ASSOCIATE'S DEGREE

Associate's degrees are two-year courses which are either vocational or the first two years of a Bachelor's programme (broad-based liberal arts). Many of these courses are done in community colleges, and students on the latter option can apply for a transfer to the third (junior) year of a university.

TRANSFER STUDENTS

Students who have completed part of a higher education course outside the USA can also apply to an American university as a transfer student. This is dealt with at the end of this chapter, and further details can be found on websites and by direct application.

PROFESSIONAL COURSES

Courses leading to a specific career are known as professional courses.

LOCATION OF INSTITUTIONS

If at all possible, you should visit any university you are considering applying to, although most institutions do not require this. Unless you have already travelled widely in the USA, it is risky to undertake such a venture without first-hand information and some knowledge of the area. The USA is, in many respects, a group of countries sharing the same language, but with cultural, environmental and other important differences between them. A small country town in America, for example, could be hundreds of miles from another town and difficult to access without transport. You could live in New York or San Francisco without your own transport, but American society relies very heavily on the car, and in many places your lifestyle will be very restricted without one. You will find that some parts of the country may be less tolerant of diversity. Climate is another issue, as winters can be extremely cold in some places and summer conditions can be extremely hot and humid for several months in other areas. If you find extreme conditions intolerable or suffer from allergies, you will need to take these factors into account. Consider therefore:

- The location of the university – is it in a large town, close to a large town or in a remote situation?
- The climate – is it temperate, or is winter very harsh or summer excessively humid?

■ The cultural aspects of the area – what activities are available; is there easy access to theatres, concerts, a wide range of shops, museums, etc.?

■ What recreational activities are possible in the area – sailing, skiing, mountaineering?

■ What are the living costs in this area? These can vary widely, with major cities and areas where the cost of real estate is high generally being more expensive.

■ Is campus accommodation available? This can vary from 100% in some private liberal arts colleges and universities to quite a low percentage in some urban areas.

SIZE OF INSTITUTIONS

■ What size is the university? This can vary enormously, and larger institutions are likely to have larger classes and may be overwhelming to some people. On the other hand, they may also offer a wider range of courses and activities.

■ The largest universities may have more than one campus and are very often in large towns. Some will be in smaller towns where the university dominates the town.

■ Smaller colleges may form a more close-knit community, particularly if they are situated in a remote area or very small town.

NUMBER OF INTERNATIONAL STUDENTS AT INSTITUTIONS

Whilst the main criteria for choosing a college will be the course and the type of institution, some students may feel more comfortable where there is either a good mix of international students or a number of other students from their own country. It is not always easy to access reliable information on a nationwide basis, but you can request this from each institution you are considering. You could also ask the EAS at the Fulbright Commission (see Appendix 2, 'Sources of information'), although they do not make such information available for publication. There are websites which rank universities according to the number of international students, but this will not tell you how many of them are from the UK. According to the Institute of International Education website, 1.4% of the international students currently studying in American universities are British. This includes all levels of study, but the majority of these are postgraduate students. India and China have the highest number of students in the USA, followed by Korea, Taiwan and Canada. The UK is 13th with 8,326 students. Numbers from countries such as Thailand, Indonesia, Malaysia and Pakistan were high, but have now dropped substantially.

The most popular destinations in the US for international students are California, Massachusetts, New York, Pennsylvania, Ohio, Illinois, Michigan, New Jersey, Florida and Texas.

Information on universities with the highest number of international students can be found in some publications (see Appendix 2, 'Sources of information' at the end of this book) and at:

- www.edupass.org – access via 'Admissions' and then 'Schoolsearch'.
- www.iie.org – access via 'Opendoors' on the home page.
- www.auap.com – produces annual rankings of universities by number of international students You need to register to access this information.

Edupass lists the top 50 schools with the most international students in alphabetical order, and highlights those which give financial aid. This can still be misleading, as some of those listed take very few international students at undergraduate level, but many postgraduates. The website also gives the top 50 schools with the highest percentage of international students, which brings in many smaller colleges, usually private, with much lower student numbers overall.

The Institute of International Education's website provides various listings, but some of these can only be accessed by subscribers. Those listed are in order of the highest number of international students, and include the top 50 for all levels of study, the top 40 for undergraduates and the top 40 for research programmes. You will notice that the undergraduate list (referred to as Baccalaureate) is very different when compared to the other two. The same, often prestigious institutions tend to appear on the total number of students and research lists, which makes it apparent that the majority of international students in these universities are postgraduates. The undergraduate top 40 tends to list less-well-known schools, with two of the top six being in Hawaii. Some very well-known liberal arts colleges do appear in the top 40, and these include Mount Holyoke College, Smith College, Wellesley College, Middlebury College and Drew University.

FRATERNITIES AND SORORITIES

Whilst many aspects of American student life may be similar to that in the UK, fraternities and sororities, together with the 'football culture' at many institutions, may be baffling to British students. Fraternities (for men) and sororities (for women) have a long tradition on the American campus, and are also referred to as 'Greek organisations' as they all have Greek names. They are national organisations and only some of them will be represented at any given university – local groups are known as chapters. You are a member of your particular fraternity or sorority for life, but the majority of people do not remain active after graduation. Students have to apply to join and there is a selection process, which finishes with a secret initiation ceremony for those accepted. There is a charge to belong, and members may live in a house owned by their chapter, or live elsewhere but have all their meals in the house. In many ways they are now social clubs which reflect the interests or backgrounds of members. Although they will usually have philanthropic aims and encourage their members to study hard (with the withdrawal of privileges if their GPA drops below a specified level) and contribute to society, there is a certain amount of scepticism, and non-supporters of the system sometimes describe them as 'partying' organisations.

It is worth finding out how strong this tradition is in any universities you are considering, as they can dominate campus life. Some colleges employ directors of Greek life who are strongly involved with student activities, and many have an office of fraternity and sorority affairs. Typically, a large public university will attract a membership of around 5% of the student body, but it could be 50% in a smaller private college. If Greek life does not appeal to you, it is worth taking this fact into consideration, as social activities could be more limited for the 'outsiders' where membership is high. Some students become heavily committed to the philanthropic activities of their chapter, some just see them as a way of making friends and having a good social life, and others find them divisive and feel they have no part on the modern campus. Members heavily involved on the organisational side feel that it helps to develop skills which will be invaluable in their future careers. You will have to decide for yourself.

The voluntary fraternities and sororities should not be confused with Phi Beta Kappa and Gamma Phi Beta, as these are 'honor societies' which only the highest achievers are invited to join. Phi Beta Kappa was actually the first fraternity and was founded in 1776.

The student in the following case study is unusual in that he started his undergraduate degree in the UK, applied for a transfer whilst on an exchange year and completed it in the USA. He became heavily involved with a fraternity, and describes the opportunities that this opened for him:

Grahaeme Hesp Transfer student, Southern Illinois University

'I have had a varied career and am now doing an EdD (doctorate of education) in Higher Education Administration at Florida State University. After working for a bank in the UK for six years I went to Sheffield Hallam University to take a degree in Business Studies, and was given the opportunity of a second-year exchange programme at Southern Illinois University, Edwardsville. I jumped at the chance as I had already done a summer camp program through Boy Scouts of America in the Southern Illinois area, where I also had relatives. As an exchange student I was on a J-1 visa.

'I lived on campus and soon became fully integrated into university life. A chance meeting led to a one-year paid internship to set up a human resources department for a bank. I wrote to Sheffield to request a year out and remained on my exchange student visa as the work counted as a practical placement. After this year I decided to remain at Edwardsville to complete my degree as I was enjoying the life so much and was heavily involved with a fraternity. As I did not have the broad range of subjects required to graduate from an American university, I had to take and pass some freshman courses and to pay the tuition fees for the final year. I sold my house in England and took out a loan.

'After graduating, I was offered the chance to do a Master of Business Administration (MBA), and paid for this partly with a 20-hour-a-week graduate assistantship. During this time I continued my fraternity work and found that I loved working with students more than doing business administration. I was still on a J-1 visa at this point and was very keen to remain in the USA – something I could only do if I did some legitimate practical training. I consulted a lawyer to make sure that I stayed within the law, and started to look for a suitable opening. I was offered a post as Director of Greek Life at a small liberal arts college in North Carolina and was able to retain my J-1 visa for eighteen months. After this, I was granted an H1-B1 visa which gave me the right to work for three years, with the possibility of renewal for a further three years. This post involved administration of the student fraternities and sororities.

'I soon realised that promotion in the USA, particularly in an academic environment, is very dependent on higher-level qualifications and that I would need a doctorate. The visa I had was no longer appropriate, so I had to return to the UK to obtain an F-1 (full-time student) visa after accepting the offer to do the EdD at FSU. Although I had some savings and received a 20-hour-per-week assistantship that provided a stipend and tuition fee waiver, I also had to take a loan.'

TIPS ■ Make sure that you are fully up to date with all the legal requirements. It is sometimes possible to find a way round some of these with legal advice, but things have changed since the terrorist attacks on 11 September 2002, and you must be aware of this.

■ Think about an exchange programme from a British university as it's a great opportunity to find out if the lifestyle suits you and to learn more about the postgraduate opportunities and graduate assistantships. The running of American campuses is heavily supported by the work of graduate students.

ADMISSION CRITERIA

AMERICAN STUDENTS

Universities accept American students on the basis of their GPA for the last three years of high school, the application form and personal statement or essay, references from teachers and counsellors and their SAT or ACT score. The GPA is recorded on an official high-school transcript which is sent directly to all universities a student applies to.

Universities will all have their own criteria for admission, as they do in the UK. The most competitive colleges may expect a high-school GPA of 4.00 and a high score in the SAT or ACT. Typically, a good public university (governed by the state in which it is located) will require a GPA of 3.25 or better on all academic subjects, together with a specified SAT or ACT score. This may sound high, but the American system does not work in the same way as in the UK, and an able student who works hard, completes all assignments and does well in the tests (mainly multiple choice) is likely to be awarded A grades on a fairly regular basis.

Students in some American high schools can now take Advanced Placement (AP) tests, which are nationally recognised and awarded by the College Entrance Examination Board (CEEB). There is a system of awarding credits for particular scores in these tests. Where these are offered, students will normally choose one subject to study at an advanced (college) level during the last year of high school and take a test in this. There is also a qualification known as the Advanced International Certificate of Education (AICE), awarding AS and A-levels, and this must not be confused with the British system. Some university guides include tables showing credits awarded for specified grades at these levels, but it applies only to the AICE which some American high schools offer.

BRITISH STUDENTS

British students are accepted on the basis of their GCSE or Standard Grade (Scotland) results, AS/Scottish Higher results and predicted Advanced Level grades, test scores (usually SAT), application form and school/college references. Many competitive colleges apply a weighting to courses and may only take into account the subjects they regard as academic. This could be a problem in the case of vocational courses since they do not readily translate to the American curriculum. A case would have to be made on the basis of the academic content of the course, and a detailed analysis of this would have to be submitted.

As the only validated qualifications at the time of application may be GCSE or equivalent examinations, you will generally be expected to have gained at least a grade B in five or more of these for admission to one of the more competitive universities. Subjects should include Maths, English, a science, a foreign language and a social science/humanities subject. The most competitive universities will have much higher requirements, and may also expect a prediction of three grade A passes at A-level or equivalent. Some of these (e.g. Berkeley) specify a minimum of grade C at Advanced Level, but will normally expect better than this. Less competitive or non-competitive colleges may accept lower grades or admit students with GCSE or equivalent only. You will normally be expected to have been in full-time education until the age of 18.

Most British students will have AS and A-levels or Scottish Higher/Advanced Higher Grades, and can apply for credits if they achieve good grades. The syllabus sometimes has to be submitted so that the content can be evaluated, and there may be a charge for this. Strong A-level results can often be substituted for the AP tests mentioned above, but you usually need to request this. At Yale University, for example, freshmen may be awarded the same credits for A and B grades at A-level as they would for top AP test scores. At some institutions, it might even be possible for students with outstanding results (AAA/AAB) to go straight in as a second-semester freshman (or even a sophomore), although they may be required to take some freshman courses in subjects they left behind at 16. Some students who are eligible to apply for exemptions, however, choose to take the full number of credits, either as a refresher course to help them to settle in and become used to the system, or to take some different courses. There are, of course, cost implications as you pay on the basis of the number of courses taken, except in some private institutions where the full fee covers as many subjects as you wish to, and can realistically take.

Whilst many of the larger institutions are familiar with AS and A-level examinations, many will not have much, if any, idea about vocational A-levels or Scottish Higher/Advanced Higher. Since the Scottish system requires students to take four or five subjects, it equates more closely to the American system of keeping a broad range of subjects open, and is likely to be acceptable when fully explained.

Similarly, if you have more specialist qualifications considered to be equivalent to AS and A-levels in the UK (e.g. a BTEC National Diploma), American universities will not be familiar with these, and you will probably have to apply to have the content evaluated by a recognised independent body if you wish to be considered for admission or claim any credits. There is normally a charge for this.

The International Baccalaureate is a highly regarded qualification that is also offered in some American schools, and most universities will use an established system of evaluation to admit students and to award credits for this.

STUDENTS WITH DISABILITIES

The United States has generally been ahead of many other countries in introducing facilities for disabled students, and you will not be disadvantaged if you have a disability. You should make early enquiries about any special arrangements.

CAN I TRANSFER FROM A DEGREE COURSE IN THE UK?

International students are generally eligible to apply for admission to a university as transfers if they have graduated from a secondary school and completed one or more semesters of full-time study at a university or other higher education institution, but some universities (e.g. Berkeley) only accept transfer students into the junior year, which requires two years of prior higher education study. Credits are not likely to be awarded at more competitive universities for subjects judged to be vocational, or if grades are below a specified level.

You would need to supply official or certified copies of all academic records and achievements, with a course-by-course evaluation, so that transfer credit can be awarded where appropriate – companies accredited to do this are listed in Chapter 4 (see 'Evaluation of your qualifications'). You would have to make individual enquiries about this as some institutions may do their own evaluation, which would simplify the process. You would also have to take the SAT or ACT tests, and may have to take freshman courses in any required subject areas that you have not studied since GCSE/Standard Grade level. There is an example of a British undergraduate who transferred whilst on an official exchange programme earlier in this chapter.

It is also possible to change to another university within the USA, but you would obviously have to go through various formalities with regard to your I-20 form and renewing your visa, and pay the associated costs. Permission is only likely to be given to students with a good academic record.

If you already have a first degree, you may find it difficult to gain acceptance as a freshman at some universities or for some courses, and should make early enquiries about this.

APPLYING TO UNIVERSITIES AND COLLEGES

HOW DO I APPLY?

You can apply to as many institutions as you wish, but should remember that there is a non-returnable fee (usually between $20 and $75) for every application submitted, so it is sensible to research your options thoroughly. There is no national application system like UCAS, and each application must be sent directly to each university you wish to be considered for, using the institution's own form, or the Common Application Form if appropriate. You may, of course, copy the same general information to all institutions, but must take care to note any specific requirements. It is a good idea to get someone (such as parents or teachers) to check everything before you send it off and to ask someone to read through your personal statement or essays. The US Educational Advisory Service offers this service and it is probably worth paying for this (currently £25 to review one essay) if you do not have anyone else who is willing, or feels able, to do it. Current British students have found the service very useful.

Applications for undergraduate courses are made to the Office of Undergraduate Admissions of each institution you apply to, in the majority of cases. Since students do not specialise until the third (junior) year, individual faculties or departments are not normally involved in the initial stage. It is important to note, however, that there are some highly specialised and competitive undergraduate courses which follow a different curriculum and application procedure. An example of this type of limited access programme is in the School of Motion Picture, Television and Recording Arts at Florida State University. Approximately 15 freshmen and 15 transfer students are admitted as film students each year, and applicants must submit the usual application form, a separate application form to the school and a 500-1,000 word essay, in addition to all the other requirements. Another example is the Creative Studies course at UCSB (University of California at Santa Barbara), where students follow a certain amount of independent study and must submit a separate additional application to the College of Creative Studies. In some cases videos will be required. You must look very carefully at all the requirements when submitting applications.

WHEN DO I APPLY?

It is important to start the application process early – at least one year in advance, which means that your research should ideally start 18 months in advance, as recommended by the EAS. Universities have different closing dates, and the most competitive will usually require earlier applications. Many of the publications and websites mentioned at the end of this book can help you with this process, but it is most important to follow the procedures laid down by the institutions to which you wish to apply. These are described in detail on websites, but make sure you follow the guidelines for international students as these will be different. You will need to make direct contact with institutions at an early stage. The US postal service can be very slow and you may wish to use FedEx or a similar service to make certain that everything arrives by the stated date. If you are quite certain that you wish to attend a particular institution you can opt to make an Early Decision, and this will constitute a commitment to that institution. This option may not be available to international students at some institutions.

THE USUAL ENTRY REQUIREMENTS

- Your completed application form and accompanying fee
- Personal statements (also sometimes referred to as essays) – including information on extra-curricular achievements. These are likely to be part of the application form
- Transcripts and certificates showing and explaining your qualifications
- Reference letters and school reports – these may be part of the application form
- Test results (SAT or ACT) – these are sent directly by test centres, but you must ensure you take the test(s) required by the dates specified
- Essays (see below) may be required for some subjects
- Certification of Financial Responsibility, to show that you will be financed for your course
- A specified level in the TOEFL if your first language is not English and you have not been educated in a British school
- Proof of completion of a high-school education or equivalent – this means that you will normally be expected to have been in full-time education until the age of 18

INTERVIEWS AND AUDITIONS

Because you are usually admitted to the university and not for a specific major, interviews and auditions are not the norm, but will sometimes be required or offered. This will be made clear on application forms and websites, and usually applies in cases of limited access and performance courses (dance, music, etc.).

THE APPLICATION FORM

The majority of institutions have their own application form which you can either request by mail or download from websites. There is, however, a *Common Application Form* currently used by 241 selective private universities and colleges for admission to their undergraduate courses. These institutions belong to a consortium of colleges administered by NASSP (the National Association of Secondary School Principals). Many institutions use this form exclusively and all give it equal consideration to their own form. If you are applying to more than one of the 241 member colleges, this gives you the advantage of only having to complete one form, which you can photocopy and send to those colleges. The application form can also be completed online (Common App Online) and sent electronically. The website (www.commonapp.com) lists all member colleges, and also provides information on current availability of freshman places, advising whether there are many places, a limited number or none. Remember that you do not specialise in a major subject for the first two years, so place availability is not subject-related as in the UK. The website also gives instructions on completing the form and lists frequently asked questions, including essay topics for member colleges. The Common Application Form is posted on the website early in July of the year prior to desired entry and removed early in June of the year of commencement. Please check websites carefully as some participating colleges also require a *Common Application Supplement* to be submitted at the same time.

You should note that separate applications may be required for specific courses (e.g. Stanford has a separate form for students gifted in art, dance, drama and music, and these students can include materials and opt for an audition).

As with all application forms, it is very important to read the entire form before attempting to complete it, and to follow the instructions carefully. You must pay close attention to closing dates, including the dates by which SAT or ACT scores need to be submitted. A registration fee is required and this must be sent with the application in $US – credit cards will usually be accepted, but otherwise a money order should be sent, unless you have a bank account in the USA. The fee is not refundable.

ESSAYS AND PERSONAL STATEMENTS

Essays and personal statements may be an integral part of the application from. Essays can refer to a statement you are asked to write about yourself and, in this respect, are similar to the personal statement required on UCAS forms in the UK. Some American universities are now using the term 'personal statement' on the application form. Many universities, however, also set or use standard essay topics to show that you have thought about an issue and can explain your views and how you reached them.

The personal statement type of essay is very important in applications to American universities, most of which stress the importance of qualities such as leadership, community service and evidence of non-academic interests. Admissions staff frequently stress that they take the 'holistic' approach and look for well-rounded students. Some university websites give quite a bit of advice on this and it is worth looking at these before submitting your application. Wabash College, for example, suggests that you ask yourself what you have done that others have not, and would like to see evidence of a passion in some area outside school (for example, music, arts, a language, collecting things or a sport). You need to think about yourself to give the reader an idea of who you are, what you think, what you've done and what you plan to do. In addition to academic excellence, Stanford, one of the top private universities, values those students who have made a significant commitment to any single non-academic area, such as athletics, music, art, leadership or community service, as well as those who have pursued a wide variety of activities.

The other type of essay commonly requested looks for an ability to think about an issue and put forward a logical, reasoned argument. This is becoming a more significant part of the selection procedure with its inclusion in the new SAT, as described later in this chapter. This type of essay will require you to take a position on an issue, and use examples to support the position you have taken. Essays are already part of the application procedure in those institutions using the Common Application Form, and you will be able to submit the same one to all those you apply to within this group. Essay topics are given on www.commonapp.com and include the option of a topic of your choice. Popular topics include the discussion of an issue of personal, national or international concern, the evaluation of a significant experience or achievement or ethical dilemma, a description of someone who has had a significant influence on you, or of a fictional or historical character or significant work or discovery which has influenced or impressed you. You would normally be expected to write between 250 and 500 words. If you are asked to fit your essay into a clearly defined space on the application form you should not exceed this. You may be asked to write on the application form and send a computer-generated copy, to make it easier for admissions staff to read. Here is an example where essays must fit the space:

Essays from Stanford University's 2004 application form

Four essays are required – the first three to fit on one side of A4 (nearest equivalent UK size) and the final one to take a full page.

- Of the activities, interests and experiences listed on the previous page (this refers to the points you have made in your personal statement), which is the most meaningful to you and why?
- Sharing intellectual interests is an important aspect of university life. Describe an experience, literary work, class, project or idea that you find intellectually exciting, and explain why.
- Jot a note to your future roommate relating a personal experience that reveals something about you.

Choose one topic from:

- 'A picture is worth a thousand words' as the adage goes. Attach a photograph no larger than 3.5 x 5 inches that represents something important to you, and explain its significance.
- 'Simplify, simplify, simplify,' intoned Thoreau. If you were to follow Thoreau's advice and scale back your possessions, what would you keep, and why?

TRANSCRIPTS OF YOUR QUALIFICATIONS

Your academic record is known as a 'transcript' in the United States, and evidence of this will always be required. Sometimes the original certificates you have gained in secondary school will be sufficient, and you may be asked to send copies with your application and bring the original certificates with you if you take up a place. Although many institutions are familiar with the more traditional British qualifications, they may still request copies of syllabuses of the work you have covered, in addition to proof of your grades. Academic records should be sent directly from your school or college, with an official seal or signed statement. Any transcripts you submit yourself will not be considered official, although you are entitled to offer an explanation of a course if you feel that this will enhance your application. The institution(s) you are applying to will make their requirements clear, and you can check them on their websites by selecting the information for freshman and international applications. If an institution is not familiar with your qualifications, they may ask you to have these evaluated by an independent organisation, and you will have to pay for this. Some larger institutions, including the University of California (all campuses), have specialists who are very familiar with AS and A-levels, and will evaluate and make offers on these at no cost to the student. The specialists at the various campuses work closely together to ensure they are making consistent judgements, as they may not be familiar with more recently introduced subjects, such as Critical Thinking.

Universities will be interested in the syllabus as well as the grades obtained, and will not necessarily give all subjects equal weighting. Although it may be possible to receive some credits for areas of work already covered at an advanced level, the broad nature of the courses for the freshman and sophomore years means that there will still be quite a number of subjects you are not familiar with, and you may be required to study some subjects you left behind after GCSE or equivalent.

If you have taken a less well-known qualification such as a BTEC National Diploma, you will almost certainly have to submit transcripts for evaluation, regardless of whether you wish to apply for credits, and you can expect to pay for this.

As has already been stated, the International Baccalaureate is widely accepted, and credits are awarded on receipt of proof of your grades for the subjects taken.

EVALUATION
OF YOUR
QUALIFICATIONS

If you wish to claim credits during your freshman year, or to transfer from another higher education or professional course, you may need to pay to have your qualifications evaluated by a recognised private company. You should clarify this when applying. If your qualifications need to be evaluated by a recognised private agency, the university considering your admission will supply the necessary forms. Services recommended by American universities include:

- Josef Silny & Associates, PO Box 248233, Coral Gables, FL 33124, USA. Email: info@silny.com; Website: www.jsilny.com
- Educational Credential Evaluators, Inc., PO Box 514070, Milwaukee, WI 53203-3470, USA. Email: eval@ece.org; Website: www.ece.org
- World Educational Services, Inc., PO Box 745, Old Chelsea Station, New York, NY 10113-0745. Email: info@wes.org; Website: www.wes.org

The following experiences are recounted by a freshman at Florida State University:

**Catherine
Balderson
Freshman, FSU,
Tallahassee**

'I decided to study in the USA after working for Camp America on a site near Boston. The camp director suggested Florida State University in Tallahassee, and I also seriously considered California State University at Long Beach after travelling around the country. I discussed the options with my parents who were supportive and agreed to be my financial sponsors. We purchased a copy of the Peterson's Guide from the US Educational Advisory Service at The Fulbright Commission in London, which gives information on the majority of degree-awarding colleges. I decided to apply for admission to FSU and was accepted after completing the application form, sending copies of my certificates and the examination syllabuses and taking the SAT. My parents also had to send a registration fee and copies of bank statements to provide evidence that I would be financially supported for my four-year degree course.

'I then had to wait for the official document (SEVIS-I-20 form) which must be presented to the US Embassy before a visa can be issued. This process took quite a long time and I found it very stressful as I didn't really know whether or not things were progressing normally. I only applied six months in advance and would advise others to apply earlier. The I-20 took a long time to arrive, and I then had to make an appointment at the US Embassy in Grosvenor Square, London, before being issued with an F-1 visa. The postal service in the USA can be very slow so we paid for the documents to be sent by Federal Express.

'I am now reaching the end of my freshman year, during which I had to take a broad range of subjects to get the range of credits required to graduate in the USA. I already had an AS level and four A-levels, including General Studies but, although I now know that I could have applied for some credits for these, this wasn't mentioned at the time so I didn't apply. I chose to major in Psychology, a new subject for me, and also had to take credit courses of my choice in Maths (Algebra and Statistics), a science (Biology and Biology Lab), a social science/humanity (Race and Ethnicity in the US), a language (American Sign Language) and English. I also had to take a music subject. Once I had been accepted, I met with an academic adviser to discuss course choices and then had to register online for each credit course. It is important to do this promptly as popular courses can fill up quickly. As my parents are paying quite a lot of money I have really applied myself to the work, and find that, provided you attend all classes and do the work assigned, it is not difficult to get good grades. So far I have a GPA of 3.5 despite gaining only 2.25 (C+) in Maths, a subject I hadn't done since GCSE. I had done very little Algebra so I had to catch up in that.

'International students at FSU are required to attend an orientation and immigration briefing in May, and my father attended a briefing session for parents at the same time. As I had to go early for this I decided to stay in Tallahassee for the optional summer school, but most American freshmen start at the end of August. I'm going home to earn some money this summer.

'As I felt it was important to get to grips with the culture and make friends, I applied to join one of the sororities and was accepted into the one I wanted. There is a one-week mutual selection process prior to being initiated into a sorority, and membership is for life. You have to pay to join, but it has been worth it for me as I now have a base where I can go to eat and enjoy social activities with other female students. It has helped me to make friends and to get used to the culture. At first I felt a bit out of it as the other girls discussed their very different high school experiences and I couldn't always relate to these. I get the impression that the high school diploma is really easy, and many of the American students are less used to study, which may be why we still have regular homework and must attend classes.

'One of the big differences I noticed was the lack of bars on campus, as the age for drinking alcohol is 21 in the USA. I chose to live in a dorm and shared a room for my freshman year (the cost was $1,300 per semester), but am moving to an apartment with friends for my sophomore year. This will be more expensive.

'Undergraduate international students are allowed to work on campus and I applied early for my social security number, but it can take months to come. It isn't easy to find work.

'I am not yet sure where I want to live in the future, but it could be difficult for me to find work in the USA as there are many Psychology students. Scientists, computer experts and nurses all have a good chance of employment, but if I decide that I'd like to stay, my only chance might be might be to marry an American!'

TIPS

■ Apply early as there can be all sorts of delays and you could miss your orientation programme, or even the start of a semester if your documentation does not come through in time.

■ Make use of the US Educational Advisory Service at the Fulbright Commission (for details see Appendix 2, 'Sources of information') as the information and advice they can offer is invaluable – if it's not possible to visit personally you can email your questions to an adviser. The library is very comprehensive – if you are not able to go there personally you can order priced publications and request free leaflets.

■ You will feel homesick at first, but stick it out and you will be rewarded. Most people are homesick for the first few weeks or even months – talk to your parents and friends, or the counsellors who are there to help you.

THE SAT (I AND II) AND ACT TESTS

There has been quite a bit of discussion about the tests used for admission to undergraduate courses in the USA as they tend to test potential rather than achievement, and rely significantly on multiple-choice questions. They are used in conjunction with knowledge-based qualifications and required by the majority of American universities, although there is a campaign to change this practice (see www.fairtest.org/ – the website of the National Center for Fair and Open Testing in Cambridge, Massachusetts). The website carries a list of some 700 colleges apparently not using the tests for selection purposes, but you must check with the institutions directly as they may still require you to take them (e.g. the California State system – different from the University of California campuses). If you check the list of colleges on this website, you will notice that there are qualifying footnotes against many of them. Some require only out-of-state applicants to take the tests, some require them only when the minimum GPA and class ranking are not met, some require only SAT II (subject tests) and some use them only for placement and academic advice purposes. Most students will find that they do need to take these tests if they want to keep a range of options open. Almost all major institutions still require them and they are never a disadvantage.

Some research has suggested that there is no correlation between SAT I scores and academic achievement, and it has been suggested that males tend to score better in them than females of similar ability. Mount Holyoke College, a highly competitive women's liberal arts college, no longer requires SAT or ACT scores, and Sarah Lawrence, a well-known liberal arts college in New York City, has recently announced that it will not require SAT or ACT scores from students graduating from high school in 2005. Other similar colleges may have made, or be about to make, similar announcements, but these are definitely in the minority, and many universities will not even consider applicants without SAT or ACT scores. You should take the SAT if you have a choice as it will be accepted everywhere.

It is widely recognised that scores can be improved by 10% to 20% with coaching, and practice papers are widely available in paper or electronic format. You should aim to get as much information about them as possible and do the practice papers. You can re-take SAT tests, but all scores are reported. There are UK-based companies and individuals offering test preparation courses, mainly for the SAT, Graduate Record Examination (GRE) and Graduate Management Admissions Test (GMAT). Details of these can be obtained from the US Educational Advisory Service (www.fulbright.co.uk/eas/studyus/tests/testtraining.html).

Most universities will accept either the SAT or ACT scores, but there is a tendency for the east and west coast areas to prefer the SAT, and the middle states the ACT. Some institutions will specify the SAT or ACT, and you will need to check the requirements of institutions you plan to apply to long enough in advance to prepare thoroughly. Several publications list the differences between these two national tests, but you should note that a new and extended SAT test is being introduced in the spring of 2005 and will be used for admission to undergraduate courses from the autumn of 2006.

A fee is payable for all tests.

THE NEW SAT I TEST
The SAT was designed to assess student reasoning, based on the knowledge and skills developed in schools, and the aim of the new

extended SAT is to improve alignment with the high-school curriculum and to add a third measure of skills to test writing ability. The scale of 200–800 for each element remains the same to facilitate comparisons. The format will be:

- Writing – this is a new section and will consist of an essay (see below), grammar and usage (multiple-choice questions).
- Critical reading (currently called 'Verbal') – shorter reading passages will be included in addition to the longer passages, and analogies will be eliminated.
- Math(s) – this will be expanded to include content from third-year preparatory Maths and quantitative comparisons will be eliminated. The sections are number and operations, algebra and functions, geometry and measurement and data analysis, statistics and probability.

The new SAT will take slightly longer, a total of 3 hours and 45 minutes. You will need to visit the website (www.collegeboard.com) for further details and for online practice tests.

The Official SAT Study Guide: For the New SAT is available from the autumn of 2004.

At the most competitive universities, the majority of students currently achieve a combined (Verbal and Math) score of more than 1310, and a score of 1010 or above will normally be expected at all competitive institutions.

SAT II TESTS

SAT II tests are subject tests, and two or three of these are frequently required in addition to SAT I at the more selective institutions. The writing test is frequently specified, but this may change with the introduction of the new SAT I. A maths subject (level 1 or 2) may also be required or recommended. Another subject can be selected from English Literature, a foreign language, a science or social studies. Some institutions specify that students who have taken the Advanced Placement (additional study in American high schools) or the IB (International Baccalaureate) will not have to take SAT II tests. This may also apply to A-levels and Advanced Higher, but you would need to ask about this.

The SAT II subject tests will continue with the exception of the writing one, which will no longer be offered after January 2005, owing to the introduction of the writing section in the new SAT I.

SAT II offers academic subject tests in Literature, US History, World History, Maths, Biology, Chemistry, Physics, Chinese, French, German, Modern Hebrew, Italian, Japanese, Korean, Latin and Spanish.

THE ACT TEST

The ACT test will also include a new 30-minute writing test for those starting undergraduate courses in 2006. This is an optional part of the test, but many major universities have stated that they will require it. Although most universities will accept the SAT or ACT, many require some SAT II subject tests as well. The ACT includes four subjects in one of its tests, but this will not replace the SAT II tests. The ACT consists of:

Science reasoning
English grammar
Vocabulary (less difficult than in SAT)
Trigonometry
Mathematical formulas
Reading comprehension

At the most selective universities, the majority of students will have an ACT score of over 29 and scores of 18 or above will normally be expected at all competitive universities.

SAT AND ACT – A BROAD COMPARISON OF TESTS CURRENTLY IN USE

- The SAT I does not include Science as this is part of the subject tests (SAT II).
- SAT I measures reasoning and ACT measures achievement.
- The Maths emphasis is on problem solving in the SAT, and formulas in the ACT.
- The ACT is generally considered to be a more straightforward test than the SAT.

■ There is more emphasis on vocabulary in the SAT and on grammar and punctuation in the ACT, but the writing addition in the SAT will change this.

■ The general emphasis of the SAT has been described as 'big-picture thinking' and of the ACT as 'attention to detail'.

Relative to SAT I, the ACT tests knowledge.

The SAT is currently scored with a guessing penalty and the ACT is not – both use multiple-choice questions, but the SAT does not use them exclusively.

You should note that a handful of selective colleges refuse to accept the ACT in lieu of the SAT, and a few may accept it only in certain circumstances. *You must always check requirements.*

TAKING THE SAT OR ACT TESTS

Check with the institutions you are applying to early – will they accept SAT I or ACT? When do the results have to reach them?

Information on registration, fees and test centres and registration forms can be obtained from the EAS at the Fulbright Commission in London (see Appendix 2, 'Sources of information'). The SAT test is given in the UK six times a year, and you should pre-register at least six weeks in advance of the registration date. You should aim to take the test in the autumn before you wish to be admitted to university. Most UK-based students take the SAT at the American School in London, but there are other centres for those living in other parts of the country. You *cannot* just turn up on the day. You will need to supply the SAT or ACT Institutional Codes for the universities you are applying to, so that your scores can be sent to them. These codes can be found in the admissions information literature.

CONTACT DETAILS

Arrangements to take the SAT in the UK can also be made with: the Educational Testing Service, PO Box 6200, Princeton, NJ 08541-6212, USA (www.ets.org) or at the European registration centre: CITO Group SAT Program, PO Box 1109, 6801 BC Arnhem, Netherlands. Payment must be by Eurocheque or international money order.

You can also register to take the test online and pay by credit card: www.collegeboard.com

For information on the ACT, contact the EAS at the Fulbright Commission or ACT Universal Testing, PO Box 4028, Iowa City, IA 52243-4028 or visit www.act.org

The ACT may be less easily accessible in the UK than the SAT.

Special services are available for students with disabilities.

LETTERS OF RECOMMENDATION (REFERENCES)

Most universities will ask for two or three letters of recommendation, including at least one from the student's school or college. Typically, an American student will be asked to submit a reference from the high-school counsellor, but it is recognised that the British system is different and you are likely to be asked for a reference from the head or principal of your school or college. If three references are required, the other two could be from two different subject teachers or one teacher and a careers or personal adviser, community worker or employer, to outline any voluntary work or particular skills you have acquired. The letter of recommendation does not necessarily indicate a separate letter, as there may be a space for references on the application form in the same way as the UCAS system.

ENGLISH LANGUAGE TESTS

If your native language is not English and you have not studied in an English-speaking country for at least one year, you will be required to provide evidence of having achieved a minimum standard, and your official test scores will have to be sent to those institutions you apply to. In the TOEFL (www.toefl.org) tests, which are universally accepted, the usual minimum score is 550 for the paper-based examination, or 213 for the computer-based test. Many universities also accept the International English Language Testing System (IELTS) with a score of seven (www.ielts.org). Some universities may require students to take their own English as a Second Language examination and, in some cases, require further study before starting the course.

5

FINANCING YOUR STUDY

The cost of your undergraduate course is a very important consideration, and it is your responsibility to ensure that you are financially prepared for the entire course. In most cases, parents or a relative will be taking on this responsibility, with supplementary money from summer vacation employment in the UK and any work you manage to obtain on campus. Universities are required by federal law to verify the financial resources of each applicant prior to issuing the Certificate of Eligibility (Form I-20 or IAP-66). You must complete the Certification of Financial Responsibility and submit it along with proof of financial support, which could be bank statements, award letters, scholarships or other acceptable evidence. You must show proof of financial support for the first year of study and demonstrate availability of funds for the entire course.

You should plan for a 10% annual increase in the cost of tuition fees, room and board and other costs, including books and insurance. Undergraduates in the USA typically spend more on books as there is usually a required reading list for each credit, and most students take four credit courses per semester. Married students will be required to show evidence of funding to support an accompanying spouse and any children.

Annual tuition fees vary from around $6,000 (extremely rare) a year to $28,000 or higher. The average for a top competitive institution is currently around $26,000, and for a good public sector college $14,000 (although American citizens who attend public universities in their home state will typically pay between $6,000 and $9,000 per annum). The cost of room and board also varies according to the location and you can expect to pay between $7,000 and $10,000 per annum. Books and insurance are likely to cost a further $1,500, and you must allow at least $2,000 for miscellaneous costs. You cannot enrol at an American university without full medical insurance and, in many cases, you will be required to participate in the university's own health insurance plan – this will be at a favourable rate and is clearly to your advantage. Most institutions have excellent student health services.

You are, therefore, likely to be asked to provide proof that you have funds of at least $25,000 per year and, in many cases, considerably more than this. Stanford advises a figure of $40,591 per year and Berkeley $35,700. Information and guidelines can be found on websites or obtained directly from any university to which you are considering applying. Remember that the cost of living is very high in cities such as New York, Boston, Los Angeles and San Francisco.

SCHOLARSHIPS A small number of scholarships are available to international students at American universities, but the majority are restricted to American citizens. The policy varies from university to university, as does the amount available. Private institutions with large endowments and wealthy alumni can typically offer financial assistance to a much larger number of students, and can choose how they distribute these funds. Stanford, for example, award international scholarships on a 'need aware' basis whilst they also award 'need blind' scholarships to home students. This means that, as an international student, you will have to

demonstrate your need for financial assistance. Stanford gives
25–30 scholarships a year to international students, who must
state from the beginning that they wish to apply for one. Harvard
awards a large number of scholarships, but it is extremely
difficult to obtain a place there.

ATHLETICS SCHOLARSHIPS

Athletics scholarships are different as the coach for each sport has a
great deal of power in deciding where the scholarships will go, and
will simply be looking for the best athletes who can also meet the
minimum academic standards. Competitive sport is much more
important in the American higher education system, where it is
often a major part of the social life in the surrounding area as well
as on campus. Games are televised, and hotel rooms are usually full
when an important match is played between rival football
(American), baseball and basketball teams.

The NCAA (National Collegiate Athletic Association) has three divisions
and over 900 universities who are full members. The standard is
extremely high, and many students have gone on to become top
international athletes. Only students with the very highest standard
are likely to be recruited at this level, and most will have competed
in national teams. They cannot, however, have professional status.
There are athletics associations for smaller colleges where
scholarships may be available and the standard will not be so high.
The amount of the scholarship varies from a few thousand dollars
to around $30,000 per year for a full scholarship.

It is important to make early contact with the athletic directors or
coaches at institutions to which you wish to apply. It is often
possible to make an initial contact with them at international
meetings if you are participating at this level. Alternatively, you can
obtain the contact details from websites (e.g. the NCAA site at
www.ncaa.org) or publications, and send in your CV (resumé) and
a videotape. Some coaches will actively recruit the top athletes, but
you should also actively seek out the opportunities yourself if you
fulfil the criteria. There is an NCAA clearing house for which a fee
is payable.

There is a limit to the number of scholarships which can be awarded in each sport and a federal law which requires that an equal amount of funding must be given to males and females. This could give an advantage to females since many sports scholars in the USA are footballers – the football played in Europe is known as soccer in the USA, and there will also be scholarships for this.

The following experiences are recounted by a student on a five-year athletics scholarship, who was the British gymnastics champion in 2001:

David Eaton Senior, University of California at Berkeley

'I first became interested in studying in America when my gymnastics club did an exchange programme with a club in Atlanta. One of the American gymnasts I met there was at Berkeley and others were at Penn State. I also met the Berkeley coach when competing in Sydney, but this was a coincidence. I looked at the NCAA website to find out where the top gymnastics teams were and emailed coaches, telling them that I was in the British team. I also sent a videotape of myself in training and in competition. I was also invited to visit Ohio State in Columbus, Michigan and Penn State, but went to Berkeley and loved it straight away. I was sixth in the British championships when I came here and became the British champion in my second year.

'After taking A-levels in Sports Studies, Graphical Communication and General Studies, I took a year and a half off and trained full time before I came to Berkeley. Normally, you have to start as a freshman in the fall semester, but I applied in October and was a spring admit. I took the SAT test in Manchester and got a combined total of 1,100 – most students here will have scored higher, but my coach is good at getting gymnasts admitted. A friend of mine at the National Training Centre in Shropshire is coming here in August with a SAT score of 960 and only one year of AS level study, but this is a first for Berkeley. There are about eight British athletics scholars at Berkeley. I had to send photocopies of all my GCSE and A-level certificates, which were signed by the head of my school, and then bring the originals with me when I came here. I also had to write a personal statement, and my English teacher and coach helped me with this.

'I didn't have any problem in getting my F-1 visa, but I did once forget to get my I-20 form signed by the International House here at Berkeley when I went home. I was detained by immigration, but they did allow me in and gave me one week to get it validated. This is not to be recommended as they could have sent me back to the UK.

'I have a very strict and disciplined routine here, with training every weekday from 12.30–4.00 pm and 7.00–8.00 pm, and a further three hours on Saturday. My classes have to fit around my training, and an athletics adviser helped me to choose the most suitable classes and major. I'm majoring in Sociology and sometimes I do have to miss classes, but lecturers can sometimes be forgiving. I did fail my first Maths test, but was able to pass Statistics so that satisfied that requirement. My other subjects were Writing, German, Social Science, Behavioural Science, Astronomy, Philosophy, American Culture, American History and American Institutions. It is possible to pass some classes by examination without attending classes, and they will provide extra tuition if you are struggling as they want you to graduate. I do have to travel a lot to compete and might miss three or four weeks. I have managed to maintain a GPA of 3.48.

'My scholarship covers tuition fees, health insurance and books, and I also get a stipend of $650 a month. As I live in a house owned by the grandparents of one of my team-mates, my rent is a reasonable $500 per month. I also coach at the gym three times a week and earn $12 per hour.

'I've seen many places in the USA through competition. I competed for Berkeley for four years (the maximum allowed) and now compete for California and for Britain. As

I was injured before the last Commonwealth Games, I'm now aiming at the next one in 2006, as we didn't qualify for the Olympics.

'I could never have come to Berkeley without gymnastics, as I'm not from an academic background and didn't work as hard as I could have at school. I now find myself in class with exchange students from Oxbridge, but through gymnastics I have learned to work hard and I now apply this to everything. I want to be involved in sport in some way in the future, perhaps working for the British Olympic Committee or for an athletics centre in a university. I would eventually like to live in America as it's been a great experience for me.'

TIPS

- Make use of the International Center or equivalent as they have all the answers to queries about status and forms and are happy to help. Make sure you get them to sign your I-20 form every time you leave the country – you won't normally get back in without it. Don't leave this to the last minute and expect them to drop everything and sign it – take it a couple of weeks in advance.
- Make sure you keep up to date with all your work to avoid letting your GPA drop. If it drops below a specified level you could be put on 'Academic Probation' and excluded from fraternity or sorority 'fun' activities if you have joined one. You could even have your I-20 withdrawn if you are not making satisfactory progress.
- Be prepared for a long wait at immigration when you enter the USA after a vacation. One student was put in a room with 50 other F-I visa students and had to wait two hours for an interview. Make sure you warn friends who may be meeting you.
- Fit in as many credits as you can at the beginning if you plan to work on campus. You'll have to wait for your social security number and will have less time to study when you are working.
- Make sure you ask to have your qualifications evaluated to see whether you can apply for any credits.
- Do your research thoroughly if you are looking for a scholarship

and take advantage of any contacts you make.

ACADEMIC REQUIREMENTS FOR ATHLETES

There has been a lot of publicity about top athletes, footballers in particular, being admitted without the academic requirements for undergraduate study. This is strongly denied by universities, and there is certainly evidence that many athletes do have strong academic credentials. At the same time, however, it is certainly possible to gain admission to a top academic institution with lower SAT scores and examination grades than would otherwise be required. You must not assume, however, that this is always the case, as many Ivy League universities, including Princeton, give no special financial or academic consideration to the athletes they recruit, on the grounds that the purpose of higher education is to enhance academic training and maturity.

Athletes are naturally expected to compete for the university in addition to their national commitments, and spend many hours training every day. Coaches tend to advise on the academic programme and frequently suggest courses in which students are not required to attend all classes, and which do not involve practical or laboratory work. When athletes are heavily involved in competition or are struggling with a course, coaches may make funds available to pay for additional help.

In addition to the most popular sports already mentioned, a reasonable number of scholarships are available in tennis, gymnastics, soccer, swimming and diving, cross country, golf, field hockey, ice hockey, track and field, softball and volleyball. A very few scholarships are available in sports such as archery, badminton, sailing, equestrian events, fencing, figure skating, skiing, rugby, martial arts, squash and water polo. Most universities will offer only the most popular sports and you will have to search websites for minority sports.

Athletes are allowed to compete for four years, although scholarships are provided on an annual basis.

The US Educational Advisory Service at the Fulbright Commission (see Appendix 2, 'Sources of information') produces a detailed free leaflet on athletic scholarships.

6

GETTING A PLACE

WHAT ARE MY CHANCES OF GETTING A PLACE?

If you can fulfil all the above requirements to at least the minimum standard, you have every chance of getting into an American university, as there are so many institutions in the USA that it is possible to find something suitable for everyone. You will need to be realistic about your chances of success, and match your academic and personal profile to those institutions to which you would like to apply. As is the case in the UK, some institutions are extremely selective and will require much higher grades. These will not, however, guarantee admission, as a great deal of attention is also given to personal statements, essays and references from teachers. Each institution has its own philosophy, and in some cases extra-curricular activities and outstanding references may outweigh high academic scores. If you feel that a particular institution is the right one for you, it is worth having a go – all you can lose is the application fee.

You should be aware that it may actually be more difficult to get into the most prestigious public universities than the most prestigious private ones. UCLA (Los Angeles) and UC Berkeley are examples of highly competitive public universities that look for entry qualifications similar to those required by Oxford and Cambridge. This is due to the large number of well-qualified applicants who are California residents and must be given priority, as the University of California is a public institution receiving funding from the state of California. Athletic scholarships are an exception to this, as many large universities, both public and private, give high priority to inter-collegiate competition, and it is a coach's job to recruit the best, regardless of their country or state of residence. Private institutions have complete freedom so far as admission of international or out-of-state students are concerned, and will be looking for those students who most closely match their criteria.

The average acceptance rate at American colleges is 70%, and 10% of students attend colleges that were their third choice or lower. Harvard and Princeton have the lowest acceptance rates at 11%, with Columbia next at 12%. Liberal arts colleges with low acceptance rates are Amherst College (Mass.) and Pomona College (California), with 18% and 23% respectively. Colleges with a high percentage of international students include Wesleyan College (Georgia) at 17%, Mount Holyoke (Mass.) at 16% and Macalester, Minnesota and the University of Maine with 15% each. This is the current position and subject to change. Remember that many highly competitive public institutions are limited in the number of students they can accept. Further information on acceptance rates can be found in the major guides and on websites such as www.usnews.com/usnews/rankguide/rghome.htm but these statistics may not be completely reliable and should be used only as a guide.

If you are thinking in terms of applying for what is known in the USA as a *professional degree* – this includes Dentistry, Medicine, Pharmacy and Law – you should write at least a year in advance. It is extremely difficult for international students to gain places on these courses and you may be required to attend an American college for a year prior to admission. The number of places on such professional courses is severely limited and it is consequently also difficult for Americans. A good Bachelor's degree in an appropriate subject is required. Some universities (e.g. Drew University in New Jersey) offer a seven-year BA/MD degree programme in which students undertake a dual-degree medical programme, but this is only open to American citizens. A SAT combined score of 1400 is required, and applicants must be in the top 10% of their high school.

WHAT ARE ADMISSIONS STAFF LOOKING FOR?

This will clearly vary, but here are the views of staff at one private and two public institutions:

Stanford University, the University of California at Santa Barbara and Florida State University.

Anna Takahashi Associate Director of Admission, Stanford

'Stanford is a highly selective institution in that admission to the university is extremely competitive. More than 19,000 students applied for a place in the freshman class in 2004. Approximately 2,400 students were admitted and the enrolling class numbers 1,640. Our international students make up about 5% of the undergraduate student population and hail from around the world.

'The international community at Stanford is extremely vibrant and dynamic – the wealth of perspectives offered by our international students is invaluable to the entire campus. Their experiences and insight add a new dimension to an environment where learning occurs through interactions with peers inside and outside of the classrooms.

'Many of our applicants prepare very *competitive* applications, and we are fortunate to be able to choose from the "best of the best." At the same time, this poses unique challenges for our staff: as admission officers, our job is to select the most *compelling* students from this highly selective pool. But what distinguishes the most compelling admit from a competitive candidate?

'The idea underlying our efforts as we evaluate an application file is "intellectual vitality." In short, we are looking for the thinking student who has a passion for learning. Our admitted students are those who have the intellectual curiosity to spark a lively and provocative discussion in a seminar and at a dinner-table conversation.

' "Intellectual vitality" is a vague term, and in many ways, that's the point. We cannot – and do not – have any mathematical formula or test that calculates whether or not a student will be accepted. That means that there are no right essay topics that will endear you to us, there are no scores that are too low for us to consider you, nor are there specific extra-curricular activities that are more important than others. Throughout the application, we want to see examples of your passion, dedication, and genuine interest in expanding your intellectual horizons.

'Beyond intellectual vitality, the additional term that resonates throughout the review process is "academic excellence." We are looking for those students who are ready for the challenges of university life, and who will take advantage of the academic opportunities available to them here at Stanford.

'Each application is read by as many as five admission officers who pass written comments to each other throughout the process. Stanford's admission office does not use a "committee" approach in our evaluations, nor does your success rely on the extent to which one staff member will "advocate" for your acceptance.

'Ours is an extremely human, compassionate, and personal process based on individual review of each application. One of the best examples of the care we put into reading every application is our commitment to "reading in context." We know that there are no two applicants in our pool who are exactly the same. We also know that each individual application demonstrates unique and diverse characteristics. Race, gender, a family's socio-economic background, life experiences, geography, age, religion, and sexual orientation are just a few of the factors that establish the uniqueness and personality of your application. Your academic record, SAT I or ACT scores (SAT II exams are also highly recommended), essays, and teacher recommendations are seen with these and many other aspects of your background in mind.

'Differences in educational systems and school environments are also noted. There are several members of the admission staff who read applications from students studying in the United Kingdom so they are familiar with schools and programs in the UK.

'Understanding your specific family background and school environment within the larger social, political, and economic frameworks of our world is perhaps the most important part of our job. At the same time, we must balance what you can bring to our campus with what others offer. We do not have any quotas for particular students or groups; instead, our job is to admit a "well-rounded class." To this end, maintaining a diversity of life experiences, backgrounds, and ideas is most critical to us throughout the admission process. We believe that spending considerable time understanding the context of each application allows us to succeed in that effort.

'There are no mathematical formulas used in the evaluation process, nor do we utilize a computer program that calculates the admission decision. We review each student's application in its entirety, and we spend considerable time understanding how all the above pieces fit together.

'Applying to colleges is a daunting process, but hopefully you will find the process to be a time of reflection that is both rewarding and enjoyable. Remember that we are always available to answer any questions you may have, so please feel welcome to contact our office.'
(See www.stanford.edu)

The University of California is a public institution with campuses across the state of California.

Mary Jacob Director of the Office of International Students and Scholars, UCSB

'The University of California system does its own evaluation of foreign academic credentials. There is no charge for this and we ensure consistency is maintained by employing specialists on each campus who confer with each other in cases of doubt. Only around 5% of our students are from outside California, and we don't actively recruit for overseas students. Private universities have more freedom with admissions, as state policies must be adhered to by public universities. I recommend the website www.edupass.org for foreign students who want to study in the USA as it contains a list of colleges indicating the number of foreign students at each, which makes it clear that these institutions welcome international students. At UCSB we currently have 11 British undergraduates and 35 exchange students. We can evaluate AS and A-levels and don't need to see a syllabus. The IB is also well known to us.

'We attach a lot of importance to the application form as we are looking for high achievers who are also well rounded, and look for evidence of extra-curricular activities such as athletics, music and community service. We encourage electronic applications and 90% of students do apply in this way. There is a common UC application form and students specify which campuses they wish to apply to. All students are required to submit an essay about themselves which is the equivalent of a personal statement. These are read by trained readers who use an established system of evaluation. We don't interview.

'The University of California, in common with most institutions, does require the SAT I (and three SAT II subject exams) and I cannot see this changing in the foreseeable future. I used to work at Mount Holyoke, one of the top all-female colleges, and they no longer use standard tests as part of the selection procedure as they prefer to put the emphasis on student achievement and believe that women can achieve more with a co-educational faculty that includes an equal number of female mentors.'

Florida State University is a public university situated in Tallahassee, close to the border of Georgia. There are currently 17 students from the UK and these are mainly postgraduates. The authors of the following two reports are not responsible for the admissions process, but act in an advisory capacity to students.

Roberta Christie until recently Director of the International Center, FSU

'We have a full cultural program and a special orientation program for international students at FSU. We help them to understand the system and give them the information they need to comply with all the regulations. All international students must show, for example, that they are covered for health insurance and cleared by our health centre before they can register for classes. They also have to show that they have access to $30,000 a year and we require evidence of this before we can admit a student. The rate of exchange varies, of course, but we ask British applicants to think in terms of £20,000 a year. Students must bear in mind that fees are subject to annual increases and they need to allow for this. The International Center has some funds it can provide to help outstanding undergraduates with tuition, but this is very limited. Students have to apply for it and we look at their grade point average. We are accessible to students who need any help, and we also offer cultural and social programmes for students and their families, and activities that bring international and domestic students together. There is a strong football culture here, but we cater for people with a wide variety of interests as well.'

The following member of staff at FSU helps to ensure that international students stay 'in-status' and to sort out any visa problems they may have.

Eydie Thurston Coordinator of International Admissions, FSU

'Since 9/11, all students require a face-to-face interview at the US Embassy or Consulate in their home country and there can be a wait of up to six weeks for this. Before they go home for a vacation they must come to us to have their full-time student status confirmed on the I-20 form. The regulations issued by immigration can change at any time and students need to refer regularly to our International Center website. There is a charge for the visa and an additional charge since the introduction of SEVIS (Student and Exchange Visitor Information System), a national database to monitor all those on F-1 and J-1 visas.

'We find that British students are very well prepared for an American higher education and can gain credits for previous study, but they need to apply for these. We operate a semester system, and classes run from August to December, January to May and June to August – the summer semester is optional, and many students choose to use this to work unless they have fallen behind with classes for any reason. As long as undergraduates complete 12 credit hours per week throughout the semester and are making reasonable progress towards their degree, they should have no problems. If they drop below 12 hours they are technically 'out-of-status' and can be put on academic probation. Classes can be taken again if necessary, and these would have to be paid for. We make every effort to help them to overcome any difficulties, but in some cases the visa may have to be revoked and they would then have to leave the country.

'International students are advised to apply a year in advance for courses as the process can take some time and the US postal service is slow. Many opt to pay for delivery of documents by FedEx.

'FSU is developing a First Friends program for international students, and this will provide new arrivals with a peer mentor to help them to settle in and encourage them to join in activities.'

7

GETTING YOUR VISA

The Immigration and Nationality Act (INA) governs the admission of all people to the United States and the rules and regulations are always subject to change. Foreign nationals can be admitted to the USA as non-immigrants for a temporary period if they wish to pursue academic or vocational studies on a full-time basis.

Full-time and exchange students in schools (universities and colleges) approved by the US Citizen and Immigration Services are eligible to apply for F-1 or J-1 visas. The F-1 visa is for full-time students (minimum of 12 credit hours a week during each semester for undergraduates) at all levels, and the J-1 visa is for exchange students who are doing part of their course at an approved school in the USA. There is a charge for visas.

ESSENTIAL DOCUMENTS

When you have been offered and accepted a place at an approved university, you will be issued with a SEVIS (Student Exchange Visitor Information System) I-20 A-B/ID form (if you require an

F-1 visa) or DS-2019 (J-1 visa) by the school accepting you. This document is your proof that you are allowed to study at the institution indicated in the United States. Before you make an appointment to take the form to your nearest US consulate, you should check to ensure that the details are correct. If they are not, you will have to contact the university for a corrected I-20. The institution admitting you will also check bank statements or other sources of funding, and make a signed statement to this effect, to prove to the consulate that you have the financial resources required for the period in which you will be in the USA. You also have to complete a visa application form DS-156 and DS-157, and males between the ages of 16 and 45 have an additional form to complete. Accompanying family members must complete separate application forms and are issued with an F-2 or J-2 visa, which does not entitle them to work. The I-20 form gives your personal details (name, country and date of birth, country of citizenship), details of the school you are attending, the title and level of the course, the date of starting the course and the latest date by which it should be completed, the amount of money required and the source of these funds. These forms must be renewed and signed by the institution every time you leave the country. New legislation requires all visa applicants to provide a biometric identifier that can be encrypted on the visa. Fingerprints and photographs are then taken every time you re-enter the USA, and these are matched to the originals.

CONSULAR INTERVIEWS

Federal policy currently requires that all visa applicants have a personal interview with a consular officer. Applicants in certain categories may be required to undergo a security clearance, but this will not normally apply to British subjects. In practice, the interviews are usually very brief, but you may have quite a long wait at the embassy or consulate. You must convince the consular officer that you intend to return to your home country after you have completed your course, and are advised to be prepared to answer questions about your reasons for wanting to do this particular course and why this degree is important to your career goals. You must ensure that all the documents required are in order, your passport is current and your photographs meet the required specifications (see Appendix 3).

EXTENSIONS TO VISAS

Extensions are possible in certain circumstances, but these have to be applied for and approved. Requests for extension forms should be completed at least 30 days before the current permission expires. The international service at the university deals with all these issues and you must report to and register with them when you arrive. You must also keep them up to date with any changes in your circumstances.

You may have to wait some time for an appointment, and a further period before you receive the visa, and should not, therefore, make any travel arrangements until you have done so.

CONTACT DETAILS

The US Embassy in London can be contacted as follows:

- Tel: 09055 444546 – these calls are charged at £1.30 per minute, but you are able to speak personally to an official. Line open from 8.00 am to 8.00 pm from Monday to Friday, 9.00 am to 4.00 pm Saturday
- Tel: 09068 200290 – 24-hour recorded information line – 60p per minute
- Fax: 020 7495 5012 – response usually within 24 hours
- Website – www.usembassy.org.uk

ON ARRIVAL

When you arrive in the United States, you should receive Form I-94 (Arrival and Departure Record) with your admission number to the United States. This number will be written on your I-20 or DS-2019, and the immigration inspector will then send the first two pages of this form to your school as a record of your legal admission to the USA. You retain the remaining pages as your proof of entitlement and should keep these in a safe place.

F-1 visa holders may leave the United States and be readmitted after absences of five months or less. When you return to continue your full-time study you must have a valid passport and visa as well as a current USCIS I-20 ID.

You can avoid any major problems at immigration if you follow the rules and remember that immigration regulations are subject to change without notice. It is your responsibility to stay informed and take the required action, and there are international specialists at all institutions to advise you and help if you do run into any problems. You must keep the staff there informed of any changes in your programme or status so that they can maintain your SEVIS record. SEVIS is an inflexible system with zero tolerance for those who violate the terms of their student status.

8

LIVING AS A STUDENT IN THE USA

FINDING ACCOMMODATION
Many students and their parents worry quite a bit about finding accommodation and you are strongly advised to start making enquiries as soon as you are accepted at a university. There will be a housing officer who can provide information about the various options and costs. In many cases, information and an application form for housing will be sent to you with your acceptance letter. In some smaller colleges, accommodation may be available for all or the majority of students, but larger universities have more limited accommodation and you may have to find private housing. As is the case in the UK, every effort is made to offer campus accommodation to freshman students who apply early enough. It is usual for students to share rooms, and this is certainly the cheapest option.

WILL I BE ALLOWED TO WORK IN THE UNITED STATES?

There are very specific federal regulations about this and you must be aware of them. International students are permitted to work for 20 hours per week on campus during the semester or quarter, and full time during breaks and the summer vacation. You'll need to get a Social Security number first and this could take some time. Off-campus employment is only permitted in the following circumstances and permission is required:

- Curricular Practical Training. Only work considered to be an integral part of your curriculum will be authorised. You must have completed a full academic year and obtain authorisation from your institution. Procedures for this will vary.
- Optional Practical Training. Only work that is directly related to your major field of study will be authorised. You will have to apply for an EAD (Employment Authorization Document) from the Bureau of Citizenship and Immigration Services. You will be issued with an Employment Authorization Card (for which you must supply an acceptable photograph) and it is only valid for 12 months. Please see the specifications for the ideal and unacceptable photographs at the end of this book. The size of the image and the pose and quality are important. Photographs can usually be cropped if the full image is retained.
- Economic Hardship. Off-campus work may be permitted in cases of sudden, unforeseen economic problems, if on-campus work is not available. You must have completed one academic year on an F-1 visa before this can be considered.

It is important to be aware that there are usually very limited employment opportunities for undergraduates to work on campus and you should not rely on being able to obtain this to fund your studies. Most international students return home to work during the long summer break.

9

UNDERGRADUATE EXCHANGE PROGRAMMES – AN ALTERNATIVE OPTION

AN OVERVIEW

As you can see, a full four-year undergraduate degree in the United States is an expensive undertaking, except for the fortunate and talented few who are able to obtain a scholarship. You may be feeling that it is not for you, perhaps because of the cost, or because you don't want to commit to four years away from your home and friends, or you have concerns about the acceptability of an American qualification. An excellent alternative option is to apply to a British university participating in a programme that offers the possibility of a year at an American university. You can find information on exchange programmes in prospectuses and on university websites. In most cases they are available to students regardless of the subject they are studying, and grades received whilst in the USA will count towards the final degree.

One such programme is the University of California's Education Abroad Programme (EAP). A number of British universities are affiliated with this programme, which offers students the opportunity to attend one of the UC campuses for the second year of their degree. The terms and conditions vary according to the home and host university but, in general, students pay only the home tuition and may also receive a small bursary. As you would remain a student of the home university, the student loan is not affected and you are, in fact, likely to be able to take a larger loan. Although a second-year student in the UK, you would take classes for third-year American students (known as upper division) and be regarded as a junior (third-year student), as this is the first year of study of the major subject. Your home university will expect you to select subjects appropriate to your degree, but you will also be free to take other classes which appeal to you. It's important to make sure that you register for classes before you go as students register online for them and they can fill up quickly. It's also important to find out about housing and sort this out in advance. Don't necessarily expect to be given this information – it's up to you to ask for it and do your own research on the university's website.

Lucy Hurst, Andrew McMaster and Chris Vinson are three of the 35 British students who have just completed an exchange programme at UCSB, and Tom Kordel completed his year at Berkeley, also through the EAP programme.

Lucy Hurst Exchange student, UCSB

'When I applied for my English with a Study in North America degree at Exeter, I was attracted to it partly because of the advertised opportunity to spend a year in California. There were also possibilities to go to Louisiana, Iowa or Kansas, but my sights were set on California. I applied through the EAP programme and had to choose three of the University of California's campuses – my other choices were UCSD (San Diego) and UCLA (Los Angeles), but I'm very happy that I got UCSB. I chose my courses when I completed the form, but didn't realise that I had to register in advance so I found that I had to 'crash' all my classes when I arrived as they were full. Fortunately I was able to sort this out, as I needed to match the English Literature courses to those I would have done at Exeter. Three of my nine classes were prescribed and I had a free choice of the others available within my major. I was also able to take Art, a subject I have always loved, and was very pleased to have a painting displayed.

'As soon as I was accepted, I had to apply for a J-1 visa (the standard visa for exchange students). I then had to go to the US Embassy in London and wait three hours for a ten-second interview! When the visa was granted, I just had my housing and travel to arrange. I live with two American freshmen in the campus village and the cost is very similar to Exeter. It's all worked out very well, but I would have liked more help in sorting out the housing as it's all done on the Internet and is a bit of a lottery. I found the process quite stressful, but managed to sort it out and sent off a letter and money order. I got a bursary of $1,000 from Exeter and $2,000 from the University of California.

'I've had a wonderful time here and couldn't be in a better place, but English certainly isn't an easy ride. In the American system you must do the reading and the homework assignments to keep up your GPA. My GPA is 3.4 (this translates to 65 or an Upper Second in the UK) and counts towards my degree. It's a lot more structured here with mid-term exams, presentations and regular multiple-choice tests, and you even get marks for participation in class discussion. In the UK you study more independently and research your topic. It's a bit more like school here. The workload is really heavy with four books to read in a week, but you are assessed more on whether you have read the book than on what you think about it. The American students of English are well read, but essay writing, although still a challenge, involves a lot less library and independent research than I experienced during my first year at Exeter.'

**Chris Vinson
Exchange
student, UCSB**

'I'm a Geography major at Durham University and wanted to do my exchange at UCSB as it's got an international reputation for geographic information systems which is my main interest. I'm taking all upper division courses, and chose to take one Geology class and the rest in Geography so that I could match what I would have done at Durham. The year will count as 40% of my final degree and my GPA of 3.91 should stand me in good stead. In the USA, a mark of around 90% is equivalent to a mark of 70% in the UK, but you do have to work hard to get the results. I find that there is much less independent learning here, and everything you do is more or less prescribed each week. I find that I'm working harder here as I have to regularly submit work based on my reading to keep up my GPA.

'The assessment techniques are completely different with multiple choice exams and continuous assessment – everything counts, including attendance and class participation. It's more like school than universities in the UK, but some of the students are of a high standard and I have some graduates in my Geology class.

'It's not all work and I'm having a great social life too – working hard and playing hard. UCSB is often called a 'party university', but there's a lot of hard work done too. I'm 19 and still under the legal age for drinking here, but quite a bit of drinking does go on within the student houses. I'm in a shared room and pay $385 a month for this. I get a bigger student loan from the UK and my tuition fees at Durham were halved for this year. I also get free health insurance under the programme.'

**Andrew
McMaster
Exchange
student, UCSB**

'I'm from Belfast and am doing a Psychology degree at York on an RAF sponsorship. I hope to become a pilot and am committed until I'm 38. The RAF really wanted me to start my pilot training after my A-levels, but I was keen to go to university and also on the idea of a year at an American university. I managed to convince them that it would be an advantage to have first-hand knowledge of the American culture, and it's been a fantastic experience. York also has agreements with the Universities of Ohio, Illinois and Toronto, but my preference was for California. Only six of the eighty students who applied for California were successful.

'After convincing the RAF I was up to scratch on my training, I had to complete an application form, write an essay, hand in my CV and have interviews with various people at York. I got my J-1 visa in Belfast and it was no problem. You have to read the information, keep an eye on the deadlines and follow the rules – the photograph, for example, must be the right size, but can be cropped.

'I live on campus and the regulations in the dorms are quite tough, with fines for any digressions. If you are caught drinking under age you have to go to AA meetings for a month. There's a lot of immature drinking here, and I find that many students haven't learned to balance work and play. The students tend to be treated more like kids than they are at home. The cost for room and board is $9,000 for the year, my health insurance is covered and I pay only the York tuition fees.

'I like the American system of starting with an undeclared major, and I find the teaching style more fun and more engaging. I'm taking upper division classes in subjects related to Psychology and also took a class in Military Science. I have to take 12 units and send back a signed evaluation form which counts towards my degree. It's important to keep up your GPA here, and you get regular tests and assessments as well as mid-term and final exams. Class sizes vary a lot and can be anything from 60 to 18, in my experience.

'I got good grades in my A-levels (AAB in Maths, Physics and Biology), but have been getting B grades here due to my extra-curricular activities. Although I'm only here for a year, I joined and became the secretary of a new chapter of a fraternity, and have been very active in setting that up with 30 other guys. We have been raising funds for causes such as the San Diego firefighters, and it's been a big part of my life. I feel that it instils a sense of responsibility and ensures you keep up your grades as you are put on social probation if you don't.'

Tom Kordel Exchange student, Berkeley University

'I'm taking a four-year MA course in Mechanical Engineering at the University of Sheffield and have just completed an exchange year at Berkeley. I chose Berkeley because it has an amazing reputation as a world-class university, the climate is far better than Sheffield, and it's so close to San Francisco (my favourite city ever). I was also offered opportunities outside California, in Illinois, Maryland and Buffalo, but didn't like the idea of a separated campus university, with no city life around.

'I had to submit a personal statement giving my reasons for studying abroad as part of the interview process to get on the EAP programme. I then had to submit university grade transcripts, A-level results, an essay detailing the reasons why I wanted to study in California and in particular at the Berkeley campus. I had A grades in my A-levels and was on course for a first-class Honours degree.

'My parents pay part of my tuition fees and continued to do so as I had to pay my regular Sheffield fees and no tuition at Berkeley. Living expenses were paid by my parents and from my student loan.

'The J1 visa application process was fairly straightforward and the interview wasn't really an interview – it just involved waiting in a queue for three hours and then answering simple questions such as why I was going and what degree I was doing.

'I had an absolutely amazing year. I had so many opportunities to travel and made loads of good American and international friends. I would love to go back and do next year at Berkeley too! I stayed at International House in Berkeley, which is so diverse that it allowed me to make friends from all over the world. It was a great experience.'

Part II

GRADUATE STUDY

10

An overview of the opportunities

There are many more students from the UK on graduate programmes than on undergraduate programmes in the USA, mainly because the range of opportunities and the prospects of employment as teaching and research assistants make this an excellent and affordable alternative. In most cases, tuition fees are waived or reduced and there is a stipend for the work done, which is generally around 20 hours per week. This means that students in American universities take longer to complete a programme, particularly in the case of a PhD or equivalent doctoral programme. This is not surprising, however, as they are also required to take courses to broaden their knowledge. Most take these in the first two years and also work for a faculty member (usually their PhD adviser). The work is not guaranteed and you have to re-apply each year, but there are usually plenty of openings, especially in the sciences.

Admission to graduate school is initially done at departmental level, and individual members of faculty have the discretion to use their funds as they see fit. These means that some students will be paid more than others and have their fees waived. The graduate teaching assistantships (known as GTAs, or GSIs – graduate student instructors) are a required part of the training for doctoral students as many will go on to teach in higher education, and this provides invaluable experience. Tasks vary, but include some undergraduate classes, discussion groups and grading of student examinations and assignments. Students whose first language is not English will be required to pass a test of spoken English (in addition to any TOEFL requirements) before becoming teaching assistants. It is common to switch to a GRA (Graduate Research Assistantship) in the later years as these involve helping with student research projects, which can be connected with their own PhD topic. Although there are more opportunities in the sciences, graduate assistantships are available in a range of other subjects, including languages, Music, Sports and Political Science. There are also some international fellowships and scholarships available (e.g. US-UK Fulbright Scholarship Programme (see 'Fulbright Commission' in Appendix 2, under 'Sources of information'). MBA students, on the other hand, will usually find themselves in fierce competition for the top schools and will have to find their own funding.

Academic researchers, particularly scientists, are part of an international community, and many work collaboratively or have links with academics in other parts of the world. Graduate students frequently receive information about opportunities through contacts of their undergraduate university department, but many also use the Internet or other sources of information to research their area of interest and track down any possible openings. Opportunities at postgraduate level are offered through the relevant department and not by the university admissions department, although they do act as an initial filter to ensure that students have what is required to get on the course. Graduate students are required to take the GRE or GMAT (for MBAs), which is the equivalent of the SAT for graduates, and will be expected to have a good Honours degree in the chosen subject. It may be possible for students with a BTEC HND to register for an MA if they get a good score in the GMAT or GRE. It is equally possible, however, that they would be required to take the final (senior) year of an undergraduate degree.

11

GRADUATE STUDENT EXPERIENCES

Ten graduate students in Florida and California (two of whom were also undergraduate exchange students in the USA) describe their experiences:

**Michael Clark
PhD student in
Political
Science, UCSB**

'I've been at UCSB for six years now and before that I was an exchange student from Essex University, based at UCSC in Santa Cruz. At Essex, I did a degree in United States Studies and I'm now doing a PhD in Political Science. The only thing I found difficult to adjust to as an undergraduate was the requirement to take three or four new courses every ten weeks. This was a burden in terms of books (cost and volume of reading). You have to stay on top of the reading, but the standard is higher in the UK. It didn't cost me anything apart from living expenses, and I got a few hundred dollars from UCSC.

'When I decided to return to the USA for my PhD I researched on university websites, applied to ten schools and was offered two places. I decided on California as I had lived here before, and I then made arrangements to take my GRE through the Amsterdam office, and actually took it online through a company near Manchester. You are issued with an F1 visa for five years, but the norm for a PhD in my area is about seven years so I had to fly back to the UK to renew it. This was after 9/11 and I had to wait four hours for an interview at the US Embassy.

'As a postgraduate, I now have a teaching assistantship, but did have to pay tuition and living expenses for the first year. I am now fully covered and, in return, do all the grading for my adviser's students and hold discussion groups around the topics of the lectures. The experience is useful and good to have on your CV. I'm now looking for a full-time job and am willing to go anywhere in the world as I've been doing international relations and comparative studies and have looked at the importance of scandals in the political arena.'

Matt Redshaw PhD student in Atomic Physics, FSU

'I was an undergraduate at the University of Surrey when I was given the opportunity of an elective period at an American university and was halfway through the third year of my four-year MPhys course (Physics with Nuclear Astrophysics) when I went to Tallahassee for two semesters to undertake an undergraduate research project in Atomic Physics at Florida State University. I was classed as an exchange student on a J-1 visa and did not have to pay tuition fees.

'At first I felt rather lonely and isolated as I saw few people outside the department, didn't have a car and couldn't buy alcohol or drink in a bar as I was still under 21. They have a strict ID policy here. I found everyone welcoming and friendly, though, and soon adapted to the life, so much so that I decided to apply to FSU for a PhD soon after returning to Surrey. The fact that I had an American girlfriend by this time was a key factor in my decision, but by no means the only reason, as I was now aware of the opportunities available for postgraduate study in the USA.

'My research project and resulting dissertation amounted to 40% of my final degree marks and gave me a keen interest in continuing in this area of work. I am now completing the second year of my PhD programme in Atomic Physics with the same supervisor I had for my undergraduate project. The course length is not well defined, but five years is average at a school such as FSU. People can finish in less time, and at some schools, such as MIT and Harvard, six years or more is the norm.

'I discovered that it is not difficult for postgraduate students in American universities to get assistantships to finance their studies, particularly in the science area. I successfully applied for a teaching assistantship, which provides tuition fee waiver and is sufficient to cover rent, health insurance, running a car and generally living in reasonable comfort. I pay tax and social security. At the end of my first year I had the option of continuing with my teaching assistantship or applying for a research assistantship. In general, students are required to teach for two semesters as part of the PhD programme and then take on research assistantships. I enjoyed teaching, but the research assistantship has enabled me to concentrate more fully on my research project. Students generally only teach for longer if there is a lack of funding from their supervisor.

'The formalities went smoothly, and I was able to apply for an F-1 visa as soon as I received official notification that I would be fully funded by the university for five years.

'It's a great opportunity which you won't regret.'

Jasmin Hutchinson PhD student in Sports Psychology, FSU

'I did my first degree in PE, Sport and Social Sciences at Loughborough University, where my major sports were netball and then rugby. I was in my final year and planning to stay at Loughborough to do an MA when I heard about an opportunity at the University of Eastern Illinois. A former Loughborough student was coaching the women's rugby team and needed some extra experienced players, and when

I was approached about this it was like a bolt from the blue as I'd never even thought about studying in the USA. I discussed it with my parents and they encouraged me to go for it as it was only for a year, fees were covered as part of a sports scholarship and paid work was available in a fitness centre. I followed their advice and have never looked back. During my MA course in Charleston, Illinois, I became aware of other opportunities in the USA, and decided that I'd like to do a PhD in Sports Psychology. I'm now finishing my PhD course at Florida State University, where I have a graduate assistantship which covers tuition and provides a stipend of $190 every two weeks for 10 hours' work per week. The work has been varied, but has included work with adult learners and coaching children with Attention Deficit Syndrome. I've supplemented this income with other campus work, as all F-1 visa holders are permitted to do.

'In Charleston I had first-hand experience of healthcare in the USA following a rugby accident in which I suffered concussion and was hospitalised. It was a shock to receive a bill for $10,000 as I hadn't really thought about the cost involved in a country without a national health service. I took the bill to the university and was relieved to hear that cover was provided as part of my scholarship.

'I am now married to an American and have applied to become a permanent resident. Until this application has been approved I can't leave the country as I'm technically 'out of status' and would not be re-admitted. I applied for, and was issued with, an EAD (Employment Authorization Document) and have accepted a job as an Assistant Professor in the PE, Health and Dance Department of Emory University, a private college in Atlanta.

'Although I never imagined in my wildest dreams that I would end up in America, it is the best thing I've ever done and I really love it here.'

Cliff Hayward PhD student in Instructional Systems, FSU

'I took a BSc in Information Technology and an MSc in Cognitive Science at Birmingham, but decided that I wanted to follow a much more applied course for my PhD and to be somewhere warmer! I approached the US Embassy and went to a talk about graduate opportunities organised by the Fulbright Commisson. I also did extensive research on the Internet and followed up a number of possibilities, both in the UK and America. The PhD courses in Britain that I was interested in seemed to be more theoretical and, although I was offered places on two, I decided to go for the more applied topic of Instructional Systems in the College of Education at Florida State University. I liked the idea of the broader curriculum offered by American universities, and the Florida climate also appealed!

'When I saw the GPA (Grade Point Average) that was expected of American students I was concerned that admissions tutors might not be aware of the different system in the UK, and sent an explanation of all my grades and what they meant in quality terms in the UK. This was not requested, but submitted as supporting evidence.

'Once I had been accepted and been awarded a teaching assistantship, I had no problem in obtaining an F-1 visa. My teaching assistantship includes working in the research lab, helping teachers with learning strategies and developing simulators. I work for 20 hours a week and get tuition fee waiver (worth $6,500 per semester) and a wage of $12.60 per hour – after deductions this leaves me with about $900 a month. I have to complete an annual tax form and get about half of the tax paid back. I don't have a car, but get unlimited bus travel within the city for a very low cost, and live within walking distance in the alumni village, where a one-bedroom apartment costs $320 a month. I can always rent a car when I need one.

'I chose to do all my course work in the early stages to leave me more time to concentrate on my research at the end. Although it has sometimes been frustrating to have to follow such a broad course, I feel that I have learned a lot of practical things. I would like to stay in America, either as an assistant professor or in a consultancy capacity.'

Elin Claridge, PhD student in Entomology, UC Berkeley

'Before coming to Berkeley to do a PhD in Entomology/Insect Biology I did a degree in Zoology at Cambridge and an MSc at the Natural History Museum in London. As an international student thinking about studying for a doctorate, it's to your advantage to first identify someone in your field of study who wants to take you on, otherwise issues like your GRE scores or lack of a GPA might be a problem. I met the professor I now work for when I did fieldwork in Hawaii as an undergraduate.

'The environment here is very different from Cambridge as the American culture is more casual and informal, and you need to be more assertive and to promote yourself. I'm employed for 20 hours a week, but living costs in the Bay area are very expensive, and I am not eligible for any financial aid or loans either here or in the UK. I can't afford a car, and 60%–70% of my stipend of $1,200 a month goes on the room I share in private accommodation. My professor pays my tuition, but many students pay this themselves. Studying in the States has been a great experience for me because I have been able to develop my own independent research project and have had funding to do fieldwork across the Pacific. The small grant opportunities to do research or attend conferences available on campus are unparalleled in the UK.

'I spent a year completing all the class requirements for my programme, and recommend looking carefully at the course requirements of any graduate programme before applying, and finding out about any financial packages offered. I had to take a qualifying oral exam before I could officially become a PhD candidate, and my tuition fee was a lot cheaper after I passed that. All I have to do now is to write up my thesis and get it approved by my thesis committee. I want an academic career and am currently looking for postdoctoral positions, either in the States or possibly in Australia. I think getting the opportunity to teach as a graduate student is a valuable experience and puts you at an advantage over European candidates applying for academic positions here in the States. Even though the political situation and regulations have changed a lot since I started my graduate programme, I still recommend the experience.'

Jonathan Hey PhD student in Mechanical Engineering, Berkeley

'I received a first-class Honours degree in Innovation and Engineering Design with French from the University of Bath. This included a work placement in France and six months at the University of Grenoble. After graduating, I spent a further year working in an engineering consultancy in the UK and Belgium.

'My father was at the University of Southampton and I talked to him and other professors about American universities. I also did quite a bit of research on websites, but the key to knowing where I wanted to go was a week-long visit, after applying, to both Berkeley and Stanford. At Berkeley, I was fortunate enough to have lunch with the professor I now work for. I also had an offer from MIT and a delayed offer from Stanford. I accepted Berkeley as my tuition was paid through guaranteed work as a graduate student researcher, and I had seen the university first hand and met my adviser. I took the GRE in London for around $120 and borrowed books of practice tests. I had to get an official translation of my degree results into a GPA and had to send transcripts from Bath as well as sending three letters from referees. I also had to supply a 'statement of purpose', which greatly benefited from both my father's and referees' feedback.

'I've just finished my first year, am still taking classes, and had to take a tough preliminary exam to ensure I could stay on the programme. I must maintain a minimum GPA of 3.3, but this is no problem as the classes are interesting. With my adviser's approval I can take classes outside my subject, and one of the reasons I came here was the opportunity to take a broad range of classes, which has been excellent. I have also found much greater flexibility with my PhD here than I would have in England.

'The number of things that I had to learn and do when applying and arriving was kind of daunting so I kept track of them and added them to a website to help other students. Some of it is specific to Berkeley, but other students will also find it useful. You can find it at: http://best.me.berkeley.edu/~jhey03/berkeley.

Richard Middleton PhD student in Geographic Information Systems, UCSB

'I graduated from Lancaster University and then did an MSc in Geographic Information Systems at Leicester. I initially went to Purdue University in Indiana, as a professor at Leicester had a contact there, but didn't settle despite the fact that this is where I met my wife! I'm now in my third year at UCSB and expect to complete my PhD in five years. The living costs are very expensive here, and I am fortunate that the department covers my tuition costs of around $4,000 a quarter for out-of-state students. I have to take classes and work as a teaching or research assistant for the professor who is my adviser. I work 20 hours a week and get $16 per hour. I do some additional research for my adviser during the summer months.

'All classes are graded and you have to maintain a GPA of at least 3.00. I didn't do particularly well in my A-levels or first degree, but got a distinction in my MSc and haven't looked back. I took the GRE on a computer at a testing centre in London, but didn't do too well in it, so I wrote to explain that British students are not used to taking these standardised tests and sent samples of my recent work.

'The recent budget crisis in California has caused more problems for foreign students, but money is available. I would advise students to work out very carefully what they want to do and perhaps take a year out. I think it's a good idea to take a Master's first. Although there is a lot of talk about the standard of students here, I find that the top 10% of undergraduates here are the same as the top 10% in Britain. I'm hoping for American citizenship in three years as my wife is American, but I'll be looking worldwide for jobs.'

Lyn Comerford MSc student in Mechanical Engineering, Berkeley

'I'm taking an MSc in Mechanical Engineering, and chose Berkeley due to its reputation, location and financial assistance available. I also looked at Michigan (Ann Arbor) and at Oxford and Imperial in England. I got a first-class Honours degree from Imperial, and this helped to secure my Anglo-California Fellowship.

'The application was done online and included a personal statement. I also had to send three references and do the GRE. The process involved in getting my F-1 visa was straightforward, but time consuming.

'My experience in America has been invaluable. I would definitely recommend studying abroad since it enables an individual to adapt to new situations and meet people from different backgrounds.'

The following case studies are written by students who are mainly responsible for their own funding. The first writer has a first-class Honours degree in Aeronautical Engineering and a PhD in Aircraft Design from Imperial College.

David Hall MBA student, Berkeley

'I raised some money from my UK bank and the rest was loaned to me by family members. It can be hard trying to raise funds for a US MBA in the UK because the banks aren't geared up to it, so I had to resort to the family finances – I had to explain to my bank what an MBA was, and then why I should do it in the US. This is a pain. There are other opportunities to get funding through scholarships, but the best way is to persuade a current employer to spend $50,000 on your education – a tough sell for non-bankers or non-consultants.

'Why did I choose Berkeley? Location, location, location – of all the top business schools it was the best location for me. I was looking to get more out of the MBA than just an academic education – I wanted the experience of northern California (sun, ski, surf) and access to the Silicon Valley community, and also applied to Stanford.

'The application process was quite long, but straightforward. Standard personal forms had to be completed, a set of five personal essays drafted to show different sides of my character, academic transcripts submitted, an interview attended (more of a two-way chat) and the GMAT taken. I found the GMAT to be less of an intellectual challenge, and more of a test to see how well you can beat the standardised system. Your time will be much better spent learning how to take the test, than brushing up on key Maths and English concepts. You don't have to be intelligent to do well because of the structured nature of the questions, but Brits are at a disadvantage because US applicants have sat similar standardised tests all their lives and know the procedure well. It's worth checking out one of the standardised test-taking books focusing on the GMAT to get a shortcut to the hints and tips that can raise your score. I should have done this a little more and taken the GMAT more seriously! Overall, US applicants do have a distinct advantage because they know the whole process. Applicants need to get lots of people to review their application to make sure all the relevant points are being presented and that each aspect of it ties in and builds on the rest.

'I had no problems with my F-1 visa, but I hear that the process is now overly complex and intimidating. Potential applicants should get used to this because that's the way the

US runs many of its official procedures for getting documentation. I spent over three hours in one airport waiting to be scanned in on the immigration department's new computer system to track student visa holders. One diamond in the rough is the International Student Service at UC Berkeley – they have been excellent in helping to navigate US non-residential alien issues!'

The following student worked in investment banks for several years after taking his first degree at London Guildhall and an MSc in Computer Science at Queen Mary College, and already had a wife and daughter when he embarked on his MBA.

**John Hopwood
MBA student,
Berkeley**

'MBA programmes are very competitive and top schools take only 5% of applicants. At Berkeley, 35% of the students are international. The course is made by the standard of the class and the strength of the faculty. The workload is very high and class participation is very important.

'I had to pay tuition fees for the entire course and did this with loans and savings, and I had to transfer money from the UK. It's difficult as the exchange rate is volatile and fees increased by 20%. You have to prove that you can support yourself for the two years and, in my case, this included moving a family here. I did manage to get a teaching assistantship and receive $1,500 a month ($7,000 a semester) for 20 hours' work a week.

'The application process was quite time consuming as I needed letters of recommendation and had to apply to my old universities for transcripts of my academic work and grades. I also had to prepare for and take the GMAT, and used a book and CD-ROM to take practice tests first.

'The university's accommodation for families is fantastic here and this has been a big help. I still have a house in London which I rent out, and this helps with the high living costs here.

'I now have a year of optional practical training and am looking for jobs in Silicon Valley. As my wife happened to be born in the USA, I'm able to apply for a Green Card, which will give me resident alien status. At the moment I can't leave the country due to the arduous process of switching from non-immigrant to permanent resident status. This is far more complicated than applying for permanent residence at the US Embassy in London.'

DIFFERENCES BETWEEN THE US AND UK SYSTEMS

The PhD students featured above highlighted the following differences in the US and UK systems:

- It takes quite a bit longer to achieve a PhD in the USA. In the UK, postgraduates doing research are not generally required to take set courses. It should be remembered, of course, that they specialise at an earlier stage and spend three years on their major subject, making it more likely that they will start graduate programmes with a more in-depth knowledge of their subject. In the USA, all postgraduate students are required to take a specified number of courses, which are usually selected in consultation with their supervisor/adviser. In order to maintain funding, a specified GPA (at least B grades) will normally have to be maintained. These courses are generally both useful and interesting, although time consuming.

- There is a difference in grading philosophy, and it is more common to get A and B grades in the US than it is to get a first or upper second in the UK. The academic work, although demanding, tends to be easier, and it is not difficult to get straight 'A' grades if you study. In the American system you will get the grade if you do the work.

- The American system is a bit more like being at school as you continue to get weekly homework assignments, even at postgraduate level. Your day is more structured and there are also regular tests.

- Almost all postgraduate students in the US work up to 20 hours a week as teaching or research assistants, which is another reason it takes longer. As well as helping to finance your course, working as a teaching assistant gives you invaluable experience –

PhDs from the US are highly regarded because of the teaching experience.

■ You have to take a test known as the GRE (or GMAT for the MBA) at a recognised test centre. Testing is online and includes Maths, verbal skills, logic/problem solving and comprehension (reading an essay and responding to questions). Different universities and courses require different scores, and results are sent automatically to any university you have applied to.

TIPS

■ It's important to start preparing early – at least a year in advance – as there are so many options and so many universities. There is a great deal of information on websites, and it is worth using them extensively to track down postgraduate courses. Don't be put off by the length of the process.

■ The opportunities for funding postgraduate study are not widely known, so make the effort to seek out the information. There are many teaching and research assistantships, especially for scientists, and these are not publicised enough. Many students are simply not aware of them.

■ As the grading system is very different in the USA (see above), it can be helpful to send an explanatory letter with your graduate school application.

■ Don't be put off by the length of the course as you learn a very wide range of skills. You may be able to complete a PhD course in three years in Britain, but in American universities you are also being paid to assist teaching and research staff, and you get a very good grounding in your subject through all the classes you are required to attend.

■ Don't be put off by having to take the GRE. It's very different from the exams usually taken in the UK and practice tests are recommended. There are many books to help you to prepare for the tests and these can be purchased from the Fulbright Commission. You can also buy a CD to test yourself before taking the official GRE, or do practice tests online.

■ If you are a postgraduate on tuition waiver, make sure that you keep up with this as it's renewable annually.

■ To keep your F-1 status you have to remain a full-time student, so you can't take a semester off as an American student might decide to do.

■ You won't feel at home immediately, but Americans are very friendly and you soon will if you give it a chance.

■ Make sure you stick to the rules and stay on the right side of the law to maintain your visa status.

■ Remember to ensure that you have all the supporting paperwork whenever you leave the country or you will have a problem getting back in.

■ Make sure you keep up with all your courses and maintain a good GPA.

■ If you are on a PhD programme, try to complete all your courses in the first two years so that you can concentrate on your research project in your final years.

■ Make good use of the US Educational Advisory Service (Fulbright). They have a vast range of information which you can order if you are unable to visit the library. You can also send them a draft of your personal statement and it is worth paying for their very helpful advice. If you have friends in the USA who are familiar with the process, you could also send it to them for advice.

■ It is worth looking at the Princeton Review website (www.princetonreview.com) and www.collegeconfidential.com as there are discussion sections for students and you can post questions.

Appendix 1

COMMON TERMS AND ABBREVIATIONS

Although you will be familiar with much of the terminology and commonly used abbreviations in the British education system, you may find those used in American college guides and in correspondence bewildering at first. Some of these, particularly concerning applications for federal or state financial assistance, only apply to American citizens and are not listed below.

ACT	American College Test – an alternative to the SAT
AP	Advanced Placement – a test for able students in some American high schools
BACU	Black American Colleges and Universities (historically, as all are now mixed)
BCIS	Bureau of Citizenship and Immigration Service (part of DHS)
CEEB	College Entrance Examination Board
CFR	Certification of Financial Responsibility
CFR	Code of Federal Regulations
CLAST	College Level Academic Skills Test
CLEP	College Level Examination Program
CPT	Curricular Practical Training (employment required as part of a degree course)

DHS	Department of Homeland Security (US Immigration)
EAD	Employment Authorization Document
EAS	US Educational Advisory Service (based at Fulbright Commission in London)
FERPA	Family Educational Rights & Privacy Act – student rights of access to and appeal against educational records
GED	General Educational Development – an alternative test equivalent to high-school graduation diploma and taken by adults applying for higher education
GMAT	Graduate Management Admissions Test
GPA	Grade Point Average
GRE	Graduate Record Examination – test for graduate admission in the USA
IELTS	International English Language Testing System
INA	Immigration and Nationality Act
LSAT	Law School Admissions Test
MCAT	Medical College Admissions Test
OPT	Optional Practical Training
OSEA	Overseas Educational Adviser
PRAXIS	Professional Assessment for Beginning Teachers
SAT	Scholastic Assessment Test – test for undergraduate admission in the USA
SEVIS	Student Exchange Visitor Information System – a national database to record and track overseas students
TOEFL	Test Of English as a Foreign Language – commonly used in the UK also
USCIS	United States Citizenship and Immigration Services
Credit Hour	The number of hours of teaching per week for each credit (subject)
Electives	Subjects which are not mandatory but award credits towards a degree
Federal	The national government
Freshman	First-year student
Greek Life	(or Greek organizations) – student fraternities (male) and sororities (female)
Internship	A period of practical training which carries course credits (see CPT)

Junior	Third-year university student (first year of major subject study)
Liberal Arts	A broad range of subjects in which passes are required to graduate
Major	Specialist subject studied intensively for the final two years
Minor	Secondary specialist subject
Public school	School run by the state (others are known as private schools)
Resumé	Curriculum Vitae (CV)
Review	To revise for examinations or tests
School	Any full-time education institution, including universities and colleges
Semester	College or university half-year (system now used by some universities in the UK)
Senior	Final year of undergraduate studies (term also applied in high schools)
Sophomore	Second-year student
State	This refers to an individual state of the USA

Appendix 2

SOURCES OF INFORMATION

A good starting point is the *US Educational Advisory Service*, a US government-funded service based at The Fulbright Commission, 62 Doughty Street, London WC1N 2JZ. The opening hours are from 1.30pm to 7.00pm on Mondays and 1.30pm to 5.00pm from Tuesday to Friday. It is not necessary to make an appointment to use the comprehensive library. If you do not live close enough to London to visit, you can order publications from them. Some of these are listed at the end of this section. It is not a placement service, but holds regular free information seminars on topics such as undergraduate study, funding and athletic scholarships, and organises pre-departure orientation sessions.
Email: education@fulbright.co.uk

There are also overseas educational advisers based in regional centres in Manchester, Edinburgh, Swansea and Belfast, offering a walk-in service only. The former three are based in university careers centres and concentrate on postgraduate study abroad. They have websites, but do not offer telephone or postal advice or information. The addresses are:

■ Manchester: University of Manchester/UMIST Careers Service, 3rd Floor, Crawford House, Precinct Centre, Oxford Road, Manchester M13 9QS. Website: www.graduatecareersonline.com

- Northern Ireland: Belfast Central Library, General Reference Department, Royal Avenue, Belfast BT1 1EA
- Scotland: University of Edinburgh Careers Service, 33 Buccleuch Place, Edinburgh ER8 9JT. Website: www.careers.ed.ac.uk
- Wales: Careers Centre, Margam Building, University of Wales Swansea, Singleton Park, Swansea SA2 8PP. Website: www.swansea.ac.uk/careers
- Ireland: The Educational Advisory Service for Ireland is based at the US Embassy Public Affairs Office, 42 Elgin Road, Dublin 4. Website: http//:dublin.usembassy.gov

Secondary centres with a limited service are based at the Universities of Birmingham, Dundee, Hull, Londonderry and Plymouth.

INFORMATION FOR INTERNATIONAL STUDENTS

- www.fulbright.co.uk – see above.
- http://educationusa.state.gov – US Department of State website which covers types and choices of institution and provides a useful checklist and pre-departure information.

COMPARATIVE INFORMATION ON AMERICAN INSTITUTIONS

- www.petersons.com/educationusa – keyword or name of institution search to locate information on colleges/courses and for details of publications listed below.
- www.justcolleges.com – includes a college directory and sample essays from leading colleges.
- www.univsource.com – select university by name, by state or by programme. Lists single-sex colleges and historically black colleges.
- www.a2zcolleges.com – facility to search for specialist colleges, non-specialist institutions offering majors subjects such as Drama, Music and Art, and colleges with religious affiliations.
- www.sourcebooks.com – publish *The Fiske Guide to Getting into the Right College*.
- www.globalcomputing.com/university.htm can select university by first letter of name or by clicking on the required state on a map.
- www.collegeboard.com/csearch – provides an A-Z of all colleges and a facility to compare up to three colleges.

- www.collegeconfidential.com – range of information on colleges and facility to post questions on the site.
- www.usnews.com, then click on Rankings & Guides – gives information on accessing rankings with regard to the number of international students, the top schools, the lowest acceptance rate, the highest graduation rate and the highest proportion of classes under 20. The site gives only the top three and then provides information on purchasing the more detailed publication.
- www.allaboutcollege.com – a site for American students which links to higher institutions worldwide. Also contains a 'college chat' facility.
- www.auap.com – produces annual rankings of US universities for international students (you have to register to access this part of the site) – offers a priced course selection service and a selection and guaranteed admission service (up to $2,000 with test fees) to UK students.
- www.universityroadtrips.com – organises North American university tours for individuals or small groups of students currently in secondary schools (includes sessions led by experienced admissions staff to guide you through the process).
- www.commonapp.org – for information on the common application form used by some institutions.

TEST INFORMATION (SAT, ACT, GRE, ETC.)

- www.princetonreview.com – section on choosing a school and preparing for the SATs with free practice test and online demo. Has an international student section. See below for publications.
- www.barronseduc.com – Barron's Educational, a publisher of many college guides and test preparation guides – see publications listed below.
- www.kaplan.com – contains information on undergraduate, graduate and professional programmes and test preparation materials.
- www.collegeboard.com – information on SAT tests and on financial aid for international students.
- www.act.org – information on ACT tests.
- www.fairtest.org – information on colleges which may exempt from standard tests.

- www.gre.org – information on GRE tests.
- www.mba.com – information on the GMAT tests.

US LIFE AND FINANCING YOUR STUDIES

- www.iie.org – click on 'Opendoors' to access lists of institutions with the most international students – site of the Institute of International Education.
- www.edupass.org – section for international students applying to US colleges. Gives sound advice on choosing a school and lists those with most international students (top 50), highlighting those offering financial aid to international students.
- www.internationalstudent.com – International Student Exchange and Study Abroad Center.
- www.prospects.ac.uk – information on study abroad for graduates.
- www.InternationalStudentLoan.com
- www.InternationalScholarship.com – searches exclusively for scholarships for international students.
- www.scholarships.com – matches students to scholarships.
- www.fastweb.com – free scholarship and college search.
- http://apps.collegeboard.com/search/advhome.jsp – search for scholarships.
- www.scholarshipexperts.com – a priced service which assists with searches for scholarships.
- www.kopia.org – a priced sports scholarship placement service.
- www.ncaa.org – the official website for athletic scholarships.
- www.finaid.org/otheraid/sports.phtml – financial aid for student athletes website.
- www.uscampus.com – covers all aspects of studying and living in the USA – includes advice on applications and getting accepted.
- www.lifeintheusa.com – a guide to American life.

IMMIGRATION INFORMATION

- http://uscis.gov – immigration services of the Department of Homeland Security.
- www.immigration.gov
- www.unitedstatesvisas.gov – a new website which is the official source of information about US visa policy and procedures.
- www.usembassy.org.uk
- www.TSATravelTips.us – the official Transportation Security Administration's site for packing tips.

INDIVIDUAL UNIVERSITY WEBSITES

The Peterson's website is an example of one which will help you to narrow down choices with a keyword search, but if you know the name or location of institutions you are interested in, you can either use a major search engine such as Google or try the common format of www. followed by the name of the institution (in full or abbreviated) and then .edu (which all end with) – examples are:

- Florida State University – www.fsu.edu
- Harvard – www.harvard.edu
- Mount Holyoke College – www.mtholyoke.edu
- Smith College – www.smith.edu
- University of California Los Angeles (UCLA) – www.ucla.edu

If you prefer to receive a printed catalogue (prospectus), this can be requested. There may be a charge.

There is also a vast range of publications and the choice can seem bewildering. Whilst they are a useful guide the statistics they contain should be viewed with a certain amount of scepticism.

SOME USEFUL PUBLICATIONS

- *10 Real SATs* – published by The College Board (see websites).
- *10 Real SAT II: Subject Tests*
- *America's Best Colleges* – *US News* – contains information on the number of international students.
- *Barron's Profile of American Colleges* – in-depth profile of more than 1,650 institutions.
- *Best College Admissions Essays* – published by Peterson's –- gives examples of successful application essays and tips.
- *Best Value Colleges* – *The Princeton Review.*
- *EAS Guide to Undergraduate Study in the US* – a free leaflet published by the US Educational Advisory Service at The Fulbright Commission (see above).
- *Foreign Students' Guide to American Schools, Colleges and Universities* – published by the International Education Service (IES) – www.ies-ed.com
- *International Student Handbook* – published by The College Board. (www.collegeboard.com) – gives admission requirements and policies for international students at over 2,500 four-year and two-year colleges in the USA.

- *Making the Major Decision* (Peterson's) – overview of nearly 2,000 four-year colleges.
- *Master the ACT Assessment* – published by Thomson ARCO.
- *Master the SAT* – published by Thomson ARCO.
- *Peterson's Competitive Colleges* – covers 433 very selective colleges for high achievers.
- *Peterson's Four-Year Colleges* – gives profiles of more than 2,100 colleges and universities in the USA.
- *SAT 1 – Sample SAT tests* – published by Barron's Educational.
- *SAT and ACT tests* – published by Kaplan.
- *Scholarships Almanac* – Peterson's – includes eligibility requirements (e.g. US citizen).
- *Sports Scholarships and College Athletic Programs* – Peterson's –- section on 'Advice to Prospective Student Athletes' lists all sports for which scholarships are available and the contact details of each coach.
- *The Best 351 Colleges* – published by *The Princeton Review*, using defined criteria.
- *The Unofficial Guide to College Admissions* (ARCO – published by IDG Books Worldwide Inc. – ISBN 0-02-863547-7). Has a section on application tips for international students and includes universities with a large number of international students and the countries most represented at each.
- *Things You Should Know Before You Go* – EAS pre-departure guide to *living and studying in the USA.*
- *Undergraduate Study in the United States* – US Educational Advisory service.

Note: Many of the above are available to purchase from, or view at, The Fulbright Commission (US Educational Advisory service) in London, although they are not always the latest editions – see above for contact details and opening hours. To order other publications consult publishers' websites for information.

Whilst guides providing details of rankings, average grading of students accepted, etc. are useful, the statistics given should be treated with a certain amount of scepticism. Do not rely on rankings of institution by quality (those which claim to list the best colleges), as there are no such official rankings, and the methodology used to assemble this data is inconsistent and subjective.

Appendix 3

US Immigration
PHOTOGRAPH SPECIFICATIONS

PHOTO FORMAT FOR NONIMMIGRANT VISA APPLICATIONS

In order to avoid delays in visa processing, please be sure your photo adheres to these new standards. You may want to take this information sheet along when you get your photographs taken.

Your photo must match the dimensions of this sample:

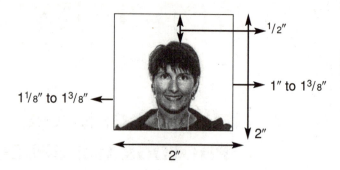

- Have you included a recent photo meeting the required dimensions?
- Is the face covering about 50 per cent of the area of the photo? In general, the head of the applicant, including both face and hair, should be shown from the crown of the head to the tip of the chin on top and bottom, and from hair-line side-to-side. It is preferable that the ears be exposed.
- Does the photo have the right dimensions? The photograph should measure 2 inches square (roughly 50 mm square) with the head centered in the frame. The head (measured from the top of the hair to the bottom of the chin) should measure between 1 inch to $1^3/8$ inches (25 mm to 35 mm) with the eye level between $1^1/8$ inch to $1^3/8$ inches (28 mm and 35 mm) from the bottom of the photo.
- Is the background white or off-white? Photos may be either in colour or black and white, but photos taken in front of busy, patterned, or dark backgrounds will not be accepted.
- Does the photo have a border? Photos may contain a small ($^1/4$) white border on *one* side of the photograph only or be completely borderless.
- Is the person facing the camera directly? (full face photo)
- Has the photo been taken within the last six months?
- Head coverings are acceptable only when the applicant's face is completely exposed.